D1372769

Mary Lincoln's Flannel Pajamas

AND OTHER STORIES FROM THE FIRST LADIES' CLOSET

"Feather Schwartz Foster has always had a fun, easy and unique way of writing about this group of women that is so near and dear to my heart - The First Ladies of the United States of America. She has an amazing ability to dig up the most interesting and rarely heard stories, and tells them in her own way, which makes them endlessly enjoyable. This latest compilation of tales is no exception."

—**Andrew Och**, The First Ladies Man, Author of *Unusual For Their Time* Contracted Producer for the C-SPAN series *First Ladies: Influence and Image*

"A delightful read. Fashion has always made a statement and the first ladies' clothing reflects not only their tastes but the times they lived in. These short stories featuring specific items such as a hat or an apron, gowns or jewelry, are both amusing and enlightening. Hats off to author and presidential historian Feather Schwartz Foster!"

—**Karen L. Schnitzspahn**, author of *Remarkable Women of the New Jersey Shore* and other books.

"There are few contemporary chroniclers of America's first ladies more adept than Feather Schwartz Foster. Her ability to penetrate the obvious and predictable has made for some endearing and revealing profiles. How comes her latest, *Mary Lincoln's Flannel Pajamas and other stories from the First Ladies' Closet*, which takes the reader deep into the persona of the women who shared their husbands (and others) with history. It's a warm and insightful look behind the scenes. You'll never again think the same of first ladies."

—**Chip Bishop**, author of *Quentin and Flora* and *New York Times* Bestseller *The Lion and the Journalist*.

"I found the stories from the First Ladies' Closet fascinating and entertaining. Fashions pertaining to First Ladies are intriguing. These fun-loving stories of the world of fashion of First Ladies are insightful and are sure to make you smile!"

—**Farron W. Smith**, Founder, Edith Bolling Wilson Birthplace Foundation & Museum

"Feather Schwartz Foster has written a unique and enjoyable book in which the personalities and demeanor of the First Ladies comes into sharp focus. Reading Foster's well-written and engaging stories about the clothing of presidential wives creates an intimate bond between the reader and these remarkable women, who lived at the center of American history. This book combines presidential and First Lady history with fashion and clothing choices, and in the process breathes new life and vibrancy into women who are sometimes forgotten or viewed as distant historical figures. And significantly, Foster's unique contribution to the literature of First Lady history also opens windows of insight into the lives of the presidents."

—**Mike Purdy**, Presidential Historian and Author at www.PresidentialHistory.com

Mary Lincoln's Flannel Pajamas
and Other Stories from the
First Ladies' Closet

by

Feather Schwartz Foster

© Copyright 2016 Feather Schwartz Foster

ISBN 978-1-63393-218-0

Images of the First Ladies were provided by the author, the Library of Congress, and Istock.com.
Illustrations by Kellie Emery

Front cover First Ladies shown:
Left (top to bottom)—Helen Taft (William Howard Taft Birthplace/National Park Service),
Ellen Wilson (istock.com)
Right (top to bottom)—Florence Harding (istock.com),
Lou Hoover (Archives & Records Administration, Herbert Hoover Presidential Library)

Back cover First Ladies shown:
Left (top to bottom)—Julia Grant (LOC), Ida McKinley (LOC), Bess Truman (LOC),
Lucy Hayes (LOC), Frances Cleveland (LOC)
Right (top to bottom)—Caroline Harrison (LOC), Grace Coolidge (istock.com),
Eleanor Roosevelt (istock.com), Mamie Eisenhower (LOC), Edith Wilson (istock.com)

Published by

◤köehlerbooks ™

210 60th Street
Virginia Beach, VA 23451
212-574-7939
www.koehlerbooks.com

Mary Lincoln's

Flannel Pajamas

AND OTHER STORIES FROM
THE FIRST LADIES' CLOSET

Feather Schwartz Foster

VIRGINIA BEACH
CAPE CHARLES

For Louise Hamilton

Table of Contents

$\mathcal{J}$ntroduction

$\mathcal{T}$here are many places where one can see clothing, accessories and other memorabilia of America's First Ladies. Many valuables, such as jewelry, remain in the individual presidential families, as they should. Presidential sites, such as Mount Vernon or Sagamore Hill, display wonderful treasures. But by far, the greatest repository of First Lady *stuff* is in the Smithsonian Institution in Washington DC, and its First Ladies exhibit is arguably its most popular venue—and has been for decades.

To keep its treasures up to date, and to include modern First Ladies collections, to keep its exhibits refreshed, and perhaps most importantly, to protect them from light, dust, moisture or other enemies of time, the Smithsonian changes its rooms periodically, and replaces and refocuses its story. It claims to have several hundred First Lady gowns and "wearables" in its keeping.

The Smithsonian is also a repository of historical knowledge, and as such, its trained scholars and experts take great care and pride in the documentation they maintain on each article. It may not matter very much to the casual visitor that a particular gown is made of x, y or z materials, but if that gown may have been the most expensive one in Mrs. President Whosis' wardrobe, it presents a human side to a First Lady.

This is exactly what this book is dedicated to doing. In my years of book signings, lectures and teaching classes, I have come to learn—perhaps to the dismay of some academics—that people want to know about the *people* who are in the history books, not merely minutiae and almanac facts, and I suspect it is because they have not been properly introduced to the great stories of history early on.

So herein, some of these early First Ladies can reintroduce themselves and their stories via an article of their clothing, whether it is a gown, a hat, a piece of jewelry, either real, or in a few cases, metaphorical, to open a window into the First Lady behind the gown.

MARTHA DANDRIDGE CUSTIS WASHINGTON

Born: June 21, 1731

Place of Birth: New Kent County, VA

Parents: Col. John Dandridge, Frances Jones Dandridge

Marriage: Daniel Parke Custis (1) - 1750

Surviving Children: John Parke (Jack) Custis;

Martha Parke (Patsy) Custis

George Washington (2) - January 6, 1759

Children: none

First Lady: 1789-1797

Date of Death: May 22, 1802

Burial Place: Mt. Vernon, VA

A $\mathcal{D}$ress $\mathcal{S}$tory

$\mathcal{D}$isplayed in a glass cabinet in the library of an old New Jersey town is a piece of iconic history. It's said to have belonged to Martha Washington, our original first lady. This historic treasure is very easy to miss, since in reality it is a pincushion. A large pincushion to be sure, tufted and shaped like a lotus flower, made from a pretty printed cloth, probably cotton or chintz. The item had been given to the library decades earlier, and the donor claimed it had been in his family for generations. It is said to have been made from one of Martha Washington's dresses. This, of course, is nearly impossible to prove definitively.

The story goes that Martha Washington had spent two winters in the Morristown, New Jersey area, where her husband was encamped during the Revolutionary War. While there, she met and was entertained by many local families, and developed pleasant acquaintances.

Many of Martha Washington's acquaintances can be verified through letters and diaries. Just as many, if not more, cannot be proven. Some people are poor correspondents. Many letters are lost over time. This does *not* mean that they did *not* exist, however, but merely that they cannot be documented.

This dress story begins shortly after Lady Washington's death in 1802, with our donor's great-great-ancestor requesting a memento from Martha's heirs, and receiving a piece of cloth that had been cut from one of her gowns. Or so they claimed.

Very few paintings of Martha Washington were executed from life, where her actual clothing is shown. Most portraits and paintings are imagined, with period-style fashions that she might have favored. The most famous of her likenesses, the one done in her older years by Gilbert Stuart, is only a head shot. Her full-length portrait hanging in the East Room of the White House today was done from imagination decades after her death.

The only hard evidence of Martha's wardrobe is her repeated purchases of American-made fabrics, begun during the infancy of the American Revolution, and which cemented her devotion to her country's cause. Woolen fabrics of brown and bottle green were colors she commonly chose for riding or traveling garments. Her formal gowns, particularly the ones from Washington's presidency, are usually described as "simple," "elegant," "unadorned," "well-made," and words befitting the consort of the Great General. The comments apply more to the quality of the fabrics rather than to the stylishness of the gowns themselves. But then again, Martha Washington was nearly sixty by that time, and *stylish* may have been unimportant.

Light printed cotton, from which the pincushion is made, is not on any list of Martha Washington's documented clothing. This does not mean it did not exist; again, only undocumented. It could easily have been a cotton day-dress or house-dress. The pattern and design was as common then as blue denim is today. Most plantation mistresses would have had several such dresses over the years. So would practically every woman of means in America.

What is interesting, however, is the *custom* of that time— cutting the clothing of the late departed for souvenirs. Martha Washington was well known and had maintained many acquaintances over her forty years as Mistress Washington. It's likely some would have requested a memento. A half-yard swatch from "old clothing," particularly one of little monetary value such as a daytime dress was a means of accommodating casual requests with little cost to the family. Items made from said fabric, such as a pincushion or pillow cover, were usually crafted to provide a practical remembrance that could be easily kept and treasured.

Fabric can be dated to determine approximate age, and one could prove that a piece of cloth could be truly from the time of Washington. It could even be determined whether the pattern was one common to that period—or not. It could just as likely have been made a generation later, in a style similar to something Martha Washington *may* have worn. But whether or not it was actually a piece of cloth from a dress worn or owned by Martha Washington will always be conjecture. We can never know for sure.

Does it really matter? Okay, how *much* does it really matter? The pincushion donor wanted to believe his family lore. The library wanted to believe their benefactor. The town residents want to believe their link to Mrs. Washington. Besides, it is a very well-made pincushion. The author is pleased to have seen it many years ago.

They don't make 'em like that anymore.

The Speckled Apron

Aprons have long been essential accessories where food— or for any work for that matter— is concerned. They are still popular today, available in all sorts of colors, materials, styles and even humorous imprints. But whether for serious cooking or for informal gatherings, they serve the same age-old simple purpose—to protect clothing.

Martha Washington likely owned dozens of aprons, albeit without funny sayings printed or stitched on them. During her lifetime, laundry was arduous, time-consuming, and followed a simple recipe: plenty of boiling water, harsh lye soap and elbow grease. It was also imperfect. Since expensive clothing could be permanently ruined by shrinkage and stains, it was much easier and more sensible to prevent the stain if possible. Thus aprons.

There is, however, an old reference to a *speckled* apron. Mrs. Washington was by that time the wife of *General* Washington, and visited him during his 1777 winter encampment in Morristown, New Jersey. Naturally the good ladies of the surrounding area were anxious to call upon such an important person and, dressed in their finest gowns and hats, they fully expected Mrs. Washington to greet them likewise.

She did not. Instead, the forty-five-year-old general's wife received them, knitting in hand, wearing a brown dress and her *speckled apron,* which seemed very informal, even borderline rude, to her visitors.

Martha Washington was very much a hands-on mistress. She was usually up before daybreak to supervise the kitchens and the regular housekeeping duties. Then she tended to the children, took up her handiwork, whether it was knitting or sewing—she was expert at both—and planned for the many guests who found their way to Mount Vernon. The dinner table was seldom set for two.

A *speckled* apron, however, suggested hard work, as opposed to a linen or lace covering. Speckled material was generally a coarse fabric. It was likely made at Mount Vernon, where spinning and weaving were important home-crafts. Martha may have even made it herself, or assigned it to any of the household women-servants who she personally taught to sew.

Who made it, or how it was made, is not the point.

The point is that Mrs. General Washington greeted new guests, the cream of Morristown, New Jersey society, wearing a coarse work apron.

Plantation Mistress

Mrs. Washington was not born and bred to be a fine lady. She was born gentry, as was Washington—comfortable, but expected to be hands-on, rather than waited on.

When she was eighteen, she married Daniel Parke Custis, a Virginia gentleman of great wealth. Both knew and sincerely cared for each other and wanted to be married, despite the fact that Custis was twice her age. It was a marriage of inclination rather than arrangement.

They were married for nearly eight years when Custis died, leaving his widow with a huge inheritance and two small children, aged four and two. The Widow Custis, now one of the wealthiest young women in Virginia, was the mistress of nearly twenty thousand acres and a workforce of three hundred, a fine home with all the trimmings of elegance, and that rarest of all colonial commodities—ready cash.

Colonial custom encouraged widowed people to remarry promptly, especially if there were small children involved. Life was hard; spouses needed spouses. The perpetual mourning traditions of Victorian times were still a century away.

When she married George Washington in 1759, Martha Custis was twenty-seven and fully capable of managing a large plantation home and its dependencies. George Washington's home at Mount Vernon was not the imposing structure that it is today. It took several years, hard work and many additions, both in the manor house and on the property, to evolve into the showplace that George and Martha had envisioned.

Thus, by the time George became "General" Washington, he had spent fifteen years building his plantation as well as his reputation. Mrs. Washington had done no less.

Even before the first shots were fired at Lexington and Concord, the colonies had supported a non-importation pact. They vowed not to purchase goods from England, relying completely on whatever they could manufacture themselves. No one took it more to heart than the Washingtons, who had long been opposed to commercial dependence on England. Martha's clothing from that time on would be American-made.

Thus Martha's Morristown guests were somewhat non-plussed at their hostess' appearance, expecting her to receive them in suitable finery befitting the General's wife. But Martha was not a lady of leisure. She knew that Washington's soldiers were a rag-tag army—hungry, sick, and poorly supplied by what was passing as central government. The individual "states" were charged with supplying their militias. This seldom happened.

When Martha came to Morristown, she had brought with her plenty of spare cloth and yarn, fully intending to put it to good use. Her days were spent knitting and sewing for her husband and the soldiers, and visiting whatever passed for field hospitals. Her hands were never idle, and she wasted no time or effort on the frills of society.

Her dress was likely plain brown. Brown and bottle green were dye colors easily and cheaply obtainable in the fledgling nation. Mrs. Washington's speckled apron sent the message she intended. As historian Paul Boller suggested, "that while the menfolk were espousing patriotism, it would be up to the ladies to espouse industry."

The message hit its mark. Thereafter, when the ladies of Morristown (or elsewhere) came to call on Mrs. Washington, they came with workbaskets in hand, prepared to sew and knit shirts and socks for the troops.

$\mathcal{A}$BIGAIL $\mathcal{S}$MITH $\mathcal{A}$DAMS

Born: November 11, 1744

Place of Birth: Weymouth, MA

Parents: Rev. William Smith, Elizabeth Quincy Smith

Marriage: October 25, 1764

Surviving Children: Abigail (Nabby) Adams Smith; John
Quincy Adams, Charles Adams, Thomas Boylston Adams

First Lady:1797-1801

Date of Death: October 28, 1818

Burial Place: United First Parish Church, Quincy, MA

Traveling Clothes

When John Adams sent for his wife, she had never been farther from home than Boston—less than twenty miles from her house.

When he and Abigail Adams married in 1764, he was a struggling attorney, riding a court circuit around Boston trying to earn a living. In the mid-eighteenth century, travel was either by foot, by horse, by horse and vehicle, or if necessary, by ship. Needless to say, it was slow and arduous. John would be gone for days and often weeks at a time.

When the politics of revolution were filling the air in the 1770s, John Adams became one of its most prominent spokesmen, and as such was named as a delegate to the Continental Congress in Philadelphia, some five hundred miles away. It took two weeks to reach Philadelphia, weather permitting, so now he and Abigail would be separated for months at a time. The letters between John and Abigail Adams flowed. During the first fifteen years of their remarkable marriage, they were apart more than they were together.

Mr. Adams Goes to Paris

In 1778, the Continental Congress, representing the newly United States of America, sent John Adams to Paris to help negotiate loans and trade for the struggling new country. The parting between him and his beloved wife would now last for another half-decade. Their letters, which had been frequent during the Philadelphia separations, would dribble to a near-halt across more than three thousand miles of ocean.

Transatlantic crossings were infrequent. The erstwhile colonies were at war with Great Britain, the mother country and world's superpower. Ships were lost. Ships were also taken as prizes. Mail packets were ceremoniously dumped into the sea once the important correspondence was confiscated. Whenever a ship arrived in Boston harbor from Europe, Abigail took the horse and wagon into town and haunted the wharves, seeking out passengers and crew, trying to learn where and how her husband was. Months could pass before Abigail even knew if John was still alive.

Abigail Adams Plans a Trip

In 1783, John finally sent for her. He had begged her to come before, but Abigail insisted she was a coward. She mostly feared seasickness, the main complaint from nearly everyone who had gone abroad.

Abigail was thirty-nine years old; her two youngest children were old enough to be left with family to complete their education. Her eighteen-year-old daughter, also an Abigail but nicknamed Nabby from birth, traveled with her. Because John Adams held an important post in his new country's government, he had instructed his wife to engage a married couple to manage their French household, as befitting his status.

So Abigail, her daughter and her newly engaged servants booked passage aboard the *Active*, a cargo ship to London that accommodated a few passengers. The *Active* carried potash and whale oil, overwhelming everyone with its stench. The journey was expected to take between four and six weeks. Cargo ships provided a means of travel but little else, so weeks of planning would be needed for such a daunting challenge.

There was a cook on board—not a very good one, according to Mrs. A.—but passengers were required to provide their own food. If fresh milk was wanted, a cow was needed. Abigail brought the cow. Dozens of chickens were provided for eggs and later butchered as they neared the end of the journey. Barrels of beer and ale, fresh water and wine were brought. Barrels of flour, of corn meal, of salted meats, of preserves, of sugar and lard. Abigail brought gallons of vinegar for sanitary and cleansing uses. She collected enough soap and candles to last for months. She also brought her medicine box of potions and powders to fend off the seasickness she justifiably feared, and would experience firsthand.

Practically assured of her personal discomfort, Abigail relied on the most comfortable clothing she had for such harsh conditions. Her finest gowns were packed away. She lived mostly in a long cotton skirt, probably in either brown or dark green, worn over a petticoat and drawstring undergarments, covered by a cotton tunic and apron—the common housework clothing of colonial New Englanders. Her shoes were sturdy, to help balance her on the ship. She spent the better part of the first two weeks in the same outfit: she became so sick that she was physically unable to change out of the clothing she had embarked with.

Passengers were also expected to provide their own entertainment—knitting and sewing supplies, books and cards, chess boards and games. Abigail also brought along French grammar books, and once their sea-legs steadied and the weather became calmer, her little party spent hours teaching themselves the language from books. She would eventually manage to read French passably, but her conversational skills would be nonexistent: no one was available to teach her pronunciation.

Mrs. Adams was assigned the best accommodations on the old ship—a tiny cabin that she separated from the crew via a clothesline draped with a sheet for privacy. And, of course, the passengers had to bring their own bedding and linens. Sanitation facilities consisted of a wooden bucket carried on deck, with a rope tied around the handle and thrown overboard for daily cleaning. No wonder Mrs. Adams had faced the voyage with dread.

As expected, the ship came nowhere near Abigail Adams' criteria of cleanliness, thus the gallons of vinegar, which also helped conceal the malodorous stench of the potash and the whale oil and close-quarter living. Abigail, Nabby and their servants tied their hair in kerchiefs, and spent hours scouring every inch of the ship, trying to make conditions more acceptable, and perhaps to fill their idle hours. They scrubbed their cabin daily, as well as the milk pail, "which had been enough to poison anybody," according to Mrs. A.

Abigail Adams Arrives in France

Five weeks later, they arrived in Paris. She had naively believed that two competent servants would be sufficient for the American diplomatic couple, and was thus amazed to find herself living in a palace with more than a dozen servants.

She had never been in a real city before. Boston, with a population of perhaps fifteen thousand, was little more than a small town. Paris was a metropolis of palaces and gardens, of magnificent buildings and avenues. She attended art galleries and theatre. She heard operas and concerts. She was initially shocked by the ballet, where the female performers wore short skirts and flesh-colored tights, but, as she wrote after she had seen several performances, "it was quite beautiful."

John and Abigail Adams spent nearly five years abroad, first in Paris and then in London. Europe proved a glorious awakening like nothing she had ever imagined. She met world renowned people she had only known by reputation, and John's occasional letters. She grew in scope and experience far more than she had ever dreamed possible.

She even acquiesced to having her hair dressed. Knowing that an important presentation at court demanded the most careful attention to the details of her appearance, Abigail decided to have her hair trimmed, styled and powdered as was the custom of the eighteenth century. She duly sent for the barber. When he arrived, he was surprised when he was brought to *Mrs.* Adams, and repeatedly insisted on seeing *Mr.* Adams. "No," replied Abigail, it was *she* who required his services, and proceeded to tell him what she wanted in a hairdo. "But I am a barber," said the confused man. "Yes," agreed the equally confused Abigail. "And I want you to arrange my hair." The conversation was obviously going nowhere, mostly due to language differences and customs. In Europe, a *barber* was strictly employed to shave a gentleman and perhaps pull a tooth. Arranging hair was done by a *hairdresser*, a separate and distinct occupation of its own.

Many of Abigail's preconceived notions of propriety and society changed during those years in Europe. Her entire outlook changed. She learned to embrace what she had always been taught to disdain. She, who had always believed heavily in *substance*, began to understand the need and value of *form* as well.

But most important of all, while she always retained her essential Americanism, she was never quite the same.

Abigail's Veils

Veils have been around since Biblical times. They are specifically a woman's accessory, designed to cover, to shield, and sometimes to hide. Sometimes they are used to tease. Even into the mid-twentieth century, veils on hats ran the up-and-down whims of fashion. Traditional brides still wear a veil at wedding ceremonies. Occasionally veils are used by women in deep mourning. Some religions prescribe them as standard dress code.

But this is Abigail Adams' *veil* story—and not even a real veil at that. It is a metaphor, and it is *her* metaphor.

Abigail Smith Adams was a Puritan New England woman, born and bred. Hers was not a life given to fashion or frivolity. Her clothes were never highly styled; she did not care for that type of frippery. Her dresses and gowns would be well made and appropriate according to the prevailing fashions—and her prevailing pocketbook—but certainly not overtly stylish.

Abigail Adams was a prolific writer, and maintained an active correspondence with both of her sisters, Mary Cranch and Elizabeth Shaw, throughout their lifetimes. Their letters were

frank, warm, informative, intelligent and delightful to read—
even today. But one of Abigail's letters is a tease.

In 1783, after she arrived safely in Paris, she wrote one sister
recounting the voyage, which was grueling, and of her initial
impressions of Europe, which was an awakening. But when she
wrote of her indescribable pleasure at seeing the husband she
dearly loved and had missed so deeply, she chose her words
carefully, employing "the poet's veil" to let her sister use her
imagination. It also ensured Abigail's modesty and gives us a
clue to eighteenth-century mores.

The *veil* letter also gives us a peek into a very private side of
the usually outspoken Mrs. Adams. Abigail's *veil of privacy* was
part of her Puritan upbringing, and would be employed many
times, for many reasons.

A Family Veil

If Abigail used the poet's veil to tease her sister about her
marital happiness, she used a similar metaphorical veil to conceal
her pain and disappointments. Some things were verboten. Not
to be shared. Certainly not to be discussed.

Abigail Adams had an alcoholic brother, albeit couched in
whatever euphemisms were common in the eighteenth century.
Alcoholism is a modern term. Medical science today provides
substantial evidence that alcoholism can be hereditary, but even
back in colonial days some suspected that it ran in families.

William Smith was the third of four children born to William
and Elizabeth Quincy Smith, and their only son. Reverend Smith
was a well-regarded clergyman and educator who strongly
believed that his daughters deserved an education as much as
his son.

Perhaps it was being surrounded by four intelligent and
unusually perceptive women; perhaps it was the old Puritan
mantra of "steady adherence to the Path of Duty, however
rigorous;" perhaps it was his early marriage yielding more
daughters. Whatever the reasons, by the time William was thirty
he was on the Path of Destruction. Intemperate and chronically
in debt, he deserted his wife and four children. Eventually he
would be involved in questionable—if not criminal—escapades

relating to forgery or counterfeiting or passing phony notes. He died at only forty-two.

Abigail, always a fond sister and ardent protector of all things family, would seldom mention his name, even within the family. Her letters to her sisters referred to "the poor man" and his follies, or "unhappy connections" and would bear the tone of her sympathy. It was such a painful subject in their correspondence that the three Smith sisters would put a mark on the envelope as a code to keep its contents *very* private. It was a shared veil.

Whether Abigail Adams believed her brother William to be possessed of a predisposition toward dissipation is unknown. However, even closer to home, there is an instance when she mentioned that she hoped her own son Charles' conduct would not "pain" his friends. It was an intuition that would bear bitter fruit.

Charles Adams, the second son of John and Abigail, was always a weaker sort. Even as a child, when the family was inoculated against smallpox, it was Charles who suffered the severe reaction while the others had minor problems. When John Adams took ten-year-old John Quincy to Europe with him, the precocious boy flourished. Wishing to do the same for his second son a few years later, the experience for both father and son would be sadly different. A very reluctant nine-year-old Charles bade his mother a tearful farewell, and was homesick thereafter. He did not acquit himself either scholastically or socially, and in the end, his well-meaning but impatient father sent him back to Abigail.

Charles eventually attended Harvard and managed to read law in New York. He later married Sally Smith, the sister of his brother-in-law—a non-blood-related William Smith that always confuses the Adams genealogy tree. Sally and Charles had two daughters.

When John Quincy was appointed Minister to the Netherlands by President George Washington, he entrusted his finances to younger brother Charles. JQ had saved a moderate sum and wanted his nest egg invested wisely. Charles, swayed by his double brother-in-law who was always on the edge of a good deal, made a foolhardy land speculation and lost his brother's entire savings.

Perhaps overcome by guilt, by dread of confession, by weakness, or all three, Charles began slipping into a repetition of his Uncle William's depredation. The slide would be a precipitous one, causing his mother's heart to "blead at every pore" for the "darling of her heart," and his father's heart to harden at what he believed were his son's character flaws. Charles died at thirty, drunk and slovenly. His widow and their two children would live permanently with Abigail and John.

Abigail's veil prevented her from committing her pen to directly address this tragedy in her life, but it is nearly impossible to ignore the depth of her anxiety and grief, which did not end with Charles.

Youngest Offspring

Thomas Boylston Adams, the youngest Adams offspring, grew up in the tumultuous times of the American Revolution, and barely knew his father, who was away for months and even years at a time.

He, too, went to Harvard and read law, although according to his mother and oldest brother John Quincy, it was "to force his inclination." Tom was never keen on law, but he acquiesced to the family profession.

In 1794, when JQ went to the Netherlands, Tom went along as his brother's secretary. He returned home in 1800 and practiced law in Philadelphia with mediocre success, but the Blue Devils, as they called it, of chronic depression that would afflict him for life had already begun to manifest. His father, the retired ex-President, urged his youngest son to return with him to Quincy, perhaps sensing his frailties, and hoping the Adams name might have professional coattails. Perhaps John had also learned a sorry lesson from his difficult relationship with Charles.

So, Tom half-heartedly entered politics and was elected to the Massachusetts legislature, but resigned a year later. He married when he was past thirty and sired several children—seven of whom would live to maturity. But his lackluster success forced them to live with his parents for many years.

While Thomas Adams proved to be an affectionate husband,

son, father, brother and uncle, he struggled with the same alcoholic demons and melancholy that had destroyed his Uncle William and his brother Charles, although it never quite spiraled so far out of control. It is also hinted that Tom had begun to gamble as well.

Abigail's veil of privacy that concealed family matters still held, but when the elderly John and Abigail made their wills, whatever inheritance left to Thomas Boylston Adams was put into a trust, to be managed by John Quincy. They did not believe that their youngest son, at forty-five, could handle responsibility.

The *Laundry* *Backstory*

Official Housing

*C*uriously enough, there was no official housing for the Vice President until the mid-*1970s*, courtesy of then-Vice President Nelson Rockefeller. Thus, Vice President Adams was obliged to provide his own residence at his own expense. For two years the couple rented a fine house in the Richmond Hill section of New York, not far from where the Senate met, and only a short distance from the presidential house on Cherry Street where Abigail could join First Lady Martha Washington at her regular levees.

During their six vice-presidential years in Philadelphia, they rented again, and entertained regularly. Nevertheless, they returned to Massachusetts often. John hated the job as Vice President, and iffy health and family cares drew Abigail back home.

But as *President* and First Lady in Philadelphia, their housing required near-constant entertaining—and the cost of food, spirits and servants was borne by the President personally, paid from his then-opulent $25,000-a-year salary. Congress, in its best wisdom, did not wish to be bothered by petty details of presidential budgets. They granted the President a munificent sum, and left the minutiae to him.

The Laundry

The White House was definitely a mansion and the largest private dwelling in the country, but it was not white. It was beige sandstone. But it was also *gratis* for the President's (*every* president's) use. It was also completely unfurnished, as was the rest of the new capital city of Washington. There were no paved streets. Workmen were everywhere, as were dogs and pigs. The snow and rain of the Washington winter mired everything deep in mud. It was cold and damp, inside and out.

First Lady Adams was no stranger to hard housekeeping. Unlike the wealthy Martha Washington, for the first twenty years of her marriage, Abigail did her own housework with no more than an occasional day-girl to help. She washed, she scoured, she cleaned and she cooked. She was also no snob, and even in her late fifties, did not object to rolling up her sleeves. Besides, there were few servants available in the new federal city.

It was to her daughter that she wrote the famous *laundry letter*. She complained about the mud and the weather. She complained about the dampness, and that they had to light all nine fireplaces to keep the place even moderately warm. Then she told her daughter about the great East Room which she had turned into a giant drying room. One can easily picture the First Lady hanging out her bedsheets and petticoats and John's drawers.

But the story continues, and this is the juicier part: Abigail and John had learned hard lessons regarding public criticism, which included an ongoing and painful exercise in remaining silent. Concerned that her obvious displeasure in the unfinished and drafty executive mansion—free or not—might reach wagging tongues, she cautioned her daughter, "but if anybody asks you, tell them we think it is lovely." John and Abigail Adams were not averse to covering a few tracks for public consumption.

Abigail's laundry letter has made history of course, and was a well-quoted and repeated story for generations.

P.S. to the Laundry Story

When Mrs. Herbert Hoover was First Lady in the early 1930s, she had a secretary who was about to be married. The First Lady decided to host a bridal shower for the young lady—in the White House. To make it special, she decided on a White House theme, and made it a *linen* shower.

She hung a clothesline across the huge East Room and when the guests arrived, they were invited to hang their unwrapped gifts of towels and sheets and tablecloths for all to see *a la* Abigail Adams!

$\mathcal{D}$OLLEY $\mathcal{P}$AYNE $\mathcal{T}$ODD $\mathcal{M}$ADISON

Born: May 20, 1768

Place of Birth: Guilford County, NC

Parents: John Payne, Mary Coles Payne

Marriage: John Todd (1)

Surviving Children: John Payne Todd

James Madison (2) September 15, 1794

Children: none

First Lady: 1809-1817

Date of Death: July 12, 1849

Burial Place: Montpelier, VA

A Quaker Fashionista

For the first twenty-five years of her life, the woman who would become Dolley Madison wore Quaker gray gowns and bonnets.

John Payne was a Quaker convert, and like many who choose their faith, was very strict in his observances. His family was raised simply on their modest Virginia plantation. Dolly was one of eight surviving children. They wore the traditional plain Quaker garb, "thee'd and thou'd", surrounded themselves with plain furnishings, and attended regular prayer meetings. It was a loving and reasonably prosperous family, but it was not particularly merry, and certainly not luxurious.

The story goes that when Dolley was ten, she was sent to stay with her *Episcopal* grandmother for a fortnight. It was there that she was first exposed to bright colors, rich velvets, lace and jewelry, rollicking music—and dessert. Dolley was completely enchanted, but all of the above was frowned upon by the Quakers.

When she was fifteen, the Paynes moved to Philadelphia, the Quaker City. At twenty-one, Dolley married Quaker lawyer John Todd who died three years later in a yellow fever epidemic.

At twenty-four, she was a Quaker widow with a two-year-old son. Then she met and married James Madison, and Dolley's life truly began.

Lady of Fashion

James Madison was not a Quaker, nor was he inclined to become one, so when the Widow Todd became Mrs. Madison, the strict elders expelled her for marrying out of faith. But Dolley didn't care. She would say more than once in her life that she never believed she had the soul of a Quaker, although she continued to wear her gray gowns and bonnet for her household chores.

James Madison came from a wealthy Virginia family. As a wedding gift, he gave his bride a generations-old necklace. Other than her wedding ring, it was the first piece of jewelry that Dolley had ever worn. He also gave her a generous sum of money to purchase a trousseau. She was happy to oblige. Bottom line: Dolley liked stuff.

The new Mrs. Madison was an attractive woman; not beautiful, but good looking and blessed with a magnetism that was, and still is, hard to describe. People would always be drawn to her. Dolley was also blessed with a sense of style. She loved bright colors, and had an innate knack for what went well together. She admired fine fabrics—satins, brocades and furs—but disdained the gaudy. She preferred classic pearls to flashy diamonds. Her tastes were simple but stylish. Her friends and acquaintances complimented her flair for fashion and emulated her choices. Her quiet husband, seventeen years her senior and half a head smaller, was grateful for his good fortune in marriage. He was happy to indulge his Dolley, and bask in her growing popularity.

The Republican Queen

When Thomas Jefferson became President in 1801, the Madisons had been married for six years and had retired to Montpelier, the Madison family plantation in central Virginia. The new President immediately recruited Madison, his closest friend, to become Secretary of State. James and Dolley moved to the brand new capital city of Washington and began their legendary hospitality.

As a city-in-situ, there were few places for government officials, elected or appointed, to meet unofficially, or at leisure. Thus the home of the Secretary of State became a mecca for gathering. The charming Mrs. M. quickly gained a reputation as the finest hostess in Washington, and her regular Wednesday evening soirées were attended by virtually everyone in town.

In 1809, James Madison was inaugurated as President and they moved into the White House. With a then-huge annual salary of $25,000 at their disposal, Dolley had a relatively free hand.

Knowing she was in the public spotlight and that everything about her would be talked about and reported, she made it a point to accentuate her role as Lady of Fashion, much as Jacqueline Kennedy would do a century and a half later. What Dolley wore was immediately copied. She liked yellow; yellow became the popular color. She favored turban hats with jewels or plumes or other ornaments, and every milliner in America began creating turban hats, with ostrich plumes as the adornment of choice. It is suggested that she favored the tall plumes because it gave her additional height to stand out in the crowd. Since her White House receptions were always crowded, the tall hat with the large feathers could be spotted immediately. One always knew where Dolley was!

Because of her personal charisma and her sense of style, Dolley could even introduce risqué French fashions. Low-cut, high-waisted Empire gowns. And rouge. And snuff for women! It would have been shocking by someone else. But if Mrs. Madison did it, it was acceptable.

Dolley Madison was called the *Republican Queen*, but not because she was queenly or remote. She was quite the opposite—warm and engaging, and remarkably democratic in social contact. She invited high- and low-brows and every brow in between, and encouraged them to mingle at will. The *queen* part came from her position in society and she was at its pinnacle. She was the one everyone followed. She took that *position* seriously. But in her inimitable way, she did not take *herself* that seriously.

Dolley returned to Washington twenty-five years later, not long after James Madison's death at eighty-five. The Widow Madison was now seventy. She was welcomed with open arms, despite the old-fashioned turbans she still wore and the one best dress she now topped with an age-appropriate kerchief. Nobody cared about that. They loved her for herself. She was still their Queen.

The *Buff Inaugural Gown*

*W*hen James Madison was elected President, Mrs. Madison was already a star of the first magnitude. Everybody knew who she was.

The two inaugurations of George Washington, one in New York City and the other in Philadelphia, had been solemn affairs. No government of the *we the people* type had ever been attempted before, and rather than rejoicing, the mood was somber and, in the Biblical sense, awesome. Martha Washington didn't even arrive in New York for several weeks.

When John Adams was inaugurated, Abigail Adams wasn't there either. She was back in Massachusetts nursing John's elderly mother, who would succumb within the month.

Thomas Jefferson, who inherited the new and unfinished White House in Washington only a month after Abigail Adams hung her laundry in the East Room, preferred the small table with a dozen or so favored guests rather than throngs. His southern hospitality was always elegant and gracious, but he was a longtime widower, as was Aaron Burr, his Vice President. Jefferson's daughter Martha Randolph was destined to be mother of eleven, and thus not always available for hostess duties. The ranking woman of Washington, therefore, was Mrs. Madison, wife of the Secretary of State. As such, Dolley was recruited from time to time to play hostess for the President, particularly if ladies were to be present.

But there was a much-needed void in the rapidly growing town, and the outgoing Dolley Madison was happy to open her own doors, providing a place for meeting, greeting, and polite politicking in an informal setting.

The Washington Social Scene

Most Washington officialdom, be they congressmen or diplomats, found accommodations in boarding houses, taverns or hotels. Few brought their wife or family. The town was little more than a village when the early presidents took up residence. Where could people meet and make introductions? Where could political men discuss the events of the day, off the record?

The parlors or salons of the fashionable and well-placed women provided the venue, and at the top of the list was the home of Secretary and Mrs. Madison. The movers and shakers of official Washington flocked *chez* Madison for luncheons, receptions, teas, dinners and suppers, which Dolley was happy to host several times a week. The socially talented Mrs. M. had a true gift for inclusion and an innate diplomacy. Even those with opposing political views could come to her parlor, certain of their welcome. She had the rare quality of counting both men and women among her many friends and admirers. Even the most outspoken or argumentative politician held his tongue lest he offend the charming hostess. All had the highest praise for Dolley. More important, that praise and those friends were sincere.

The First Inaugural Ball and Ball Gown

By 1809, when James Madison was inaugurated, Washington had grown substantially, as had the country, which was now celebrating its twentieth birthday as a government. Always ready for a party, Mrs. Madison decided that an Inaugural Ball at Long's Hotel near the Capitol would commemorate the occasion very nicely. More than three hundred invitations were issued, the largest number of guests ever seen at an event in the city. Caterers and confectioners were hired. Musicians were engaged. Decorations were hung and hundreds of candles lit the room. Everybody who was anybody in Washington came in their finery to make merry, to dance, to dine and to enjoy.

Dolley outdid herself, dazzling in her buff-colored gown and matching turban with feather plumes. Both buff and turbans immediately became the fashion of the day. At only forty, she was at the pinnacle of her physical beauty, considered more handsome than beautiful. She was of medium height and build, somewhat taller and heavier than her slight husband, James Madison, whose height is variously recorded between five-foot and five-foot six-inches. His weight, however, never was recorded to exceed one hundred twenty-five pounds.

Wearing her inaugural gown, *sans turban*, the new First Lady was commemorated in a magnificent painting by Gilbert Stuart, the most prominent portrait artist of his time. It may not be as famous as his portraits of George and Martha Washington, but it is surely among his loveliest—Dolley, in her buff-colored empire gown with the low neckline and gold trim, was the quintessential Mrs. Madison. And Stuart's artist eye completely captured her blue eyes expressing warmth and welcome.

The *coup de grace*, however, was not Dolley's outfit. That came at the supper. Dolley Madison, as was her custom, sat at the head of the table, relieving her quiet husband of hosting and serving responsibilities. To one side of the new First Lady sat the Minister of France, and on the other, the Minister of England. Their countries were currently at war, traditional enemies for centuries. Under any other circumstances, the two ministers would not have even been in the same room together, let alone at the same table. But they both liked and admired Mrs. Madison, and would not wish to offend her. Only Dolley could have managed that diplomatic feat. And in Dolley Madison's case, it was truly the woman behind the gown that made the impression.

And the Inaugural Ball has become a quadrennial tradition for two centuries.

Turban Hats

The handful of images of Dolley Madison, whether painted or etched from life or created from later imagination, usually features her in a turban-style hat. It was her trademark, and would be fashionable for more than a decade in the early nineteenth century.

It wasn't so much the turban itself but the wearer who attracted the style, much like Jacqueline Kennedy's little pillbox hats a hundred and fifty years later. Dolley Madison was such a charismatic personage that she could have worn a flowerpot and it would have been all the rage. For a Quaker girl born and raised, this was a huge departure from her upbringing, but Dolley would remark more than once that she did not have the soul of a Quaker. She liked the fluff and fashion.

Hats. Period.

Until the mid-twentieth century, head coverings had always been an essential part of a woman's wardrobe, and no lady would dream of being out in public without wearing one. They even wore caps indoors. Every woman in every station in life had a hat. Most had more than one. Every age created its own fashion style, and the muslin or lace *mob caps* of colonial times would make way for the large and fancifully decorated Gainsborough hats, and again to the imposing turbans that Dolley Madison favored. They, in turn, would fashion into beribboned bonnets of the mid-nineteenth century.

Whether the actual turban style was designed and adapted to commemorate the victorious North Africa Barbary Coast wars of the early Jefferson presidency, or merely coincidental, the draped soft material fashioned into a woman's hat was the one First Lady Dolley Madison liked best. And such was her fashion sense and her genuine popularity, that the hats were copied and emulated. Every milliner in the country made them.

Noted Dolley historian and scholar Catherine Allgor claims turbans gave Mrs. Madison added visibility in a crowded room. Dolley was average size, but with a higher heel and a high turban hat, she added several inches. A bright yellow or white turban, adorned with an ostrich or egret plume would easily be spotted and one could always find the hostess.

Dolley Madison wore those trademark turban hats until her dying day, long after her tenure in the White House ended and ladies' fashions in hats yielded to newer styles. The few existing photographs—a new invention in Dolley's old age—show the elderly Mrs. M. wearing one of her old turban hats, *sans* plumes.

The Old Clothes Story

Dolley Madison's retirement years were far from golden. In 1817, the former First Lady and President Madison retired to Montpelier, his family plantation in central Virginia. They remained there for the next twenty years. Then Madison, last of our Founding Fathers, died at the ripe old age of eighty-five.

Dolley Madison was seventeen years younger than her husband, nearly seventy herself when he died. Her health was generally good, but age being what it is and the state of medical science being what it was in 1836, she had aches, pains, creaks and groans.

Those twenty years of retirement at Montpelier were vastly different than Dolley's life at the center of Washington society. While guests were frequent at Montpelier, and always welcomed with warm Southern hospitality, the former First Lady no longer needed an expensive or extensive wardrobe. Her old gowns could easily be reworked for additional service.

One of the interesting things about Dolley is that she appears to have maintained her size. The few photographs of her in elder years depict a woman about the same height and weight as she had been decades earlier. If she wore her old clothes, she was fortunate that gravity was kind. They still fit.

Maintaining Montpelier, however, was overwhelming. It had been too much for her husband to handle in his waning years, and in truth, it had become rundown and unprofitable. Complicating the financial burdens associated with the general vagaries of farming was the dissipation of Dolley's son, Payne Todd. Payne had been two years old when a recently widowed Dolley married James Madison. Payne was good-looking and charming like his mother, and had been given every advantage. But he was lazy. By twenty, he had become addicted to wine, women and wagering. Over the years, his gentle stepfather spent more than $80,000 to cover Payne's debts. Dolley only knew a fraction of the problem.

She decided to sell the plantation.

About a year after Madison's death, Dolley returned to Washington, a place she hadn't seen for twenty years. It had changed dramatically. The small village was now a substantial town, with shops and hotels and restaurants and hundreds of homes. Happily for the Widow Madison, many of the people she had known years ago were still there. It was an easy readjustment for her—except financially. She had very little to live on, once all the Madison debts had been paid. But despite her inability to entertain as often and as magnificently as she had once done, she was invited everywhere. It was said that no gathering in Washington was official without the Divine Mrs. M.

By the 1840s, photography had been invented. A photograph was *exactly* how you looked. You no longer depended on the talents of a portrait artist. All the important people in Washington wanted to pose for the camera, as well as for posterity. Mrs. Madison was one of the most important people in Washington, truly a national treasure, and was thus photographed on a few occasions during her later years. The photographs were taken at different times, sometimes a couple of years apart, and at different locations. But the old gown and the old turban hat appear to be the same in every photograph. It is likely her best dress, the one she wore for every important occasion.

It is a black gown, and appropriate. After all, Mrs. Madison was a widow in her seventies. It may have always been a black gown, since mourning clothing was usually part of every woman's wardrobe. Maybe not. Dolley had always loved color, and her First Lady wardrobe had been a virtual palette of high shades. The gown may well have been dyed at some point; the colors may have faded. And, as people tend to grow older, bright shades are often harsh and undignified. It is also apparent from the photographs, that the elderly woman had added a decorous white kerchief to cover a neckline that was no longer in fashion, giving added consideration to the possibility of a dyed gown. Mourning clothing usually features very prim necklines. Dolley had always been fashionable, but she was no fool. She knew that at that certain stage of life, *appropriate* beats *fashion* every time.

But the white turban hat was likely untouched. Styles had come and gone. The turban hats she had popularized forty years earlier had given way to bonnets with ribbons and florets and bows tied under the chin. The Widow Dolley needed to put food on her table, and could only open her small rented house to guests once a month. A new bonnet for the sake of style was out of the question. The white turban would have to do a little longer.

Dolley's clothes were old and out of fashion, but Dolley herself was not. She was still as popular and beloved as she had always been, and even continued to make new friends. So if her clothes were the same she had worn for years, nobody cared and nobody gossiped about that dowdy Mrs. Madison. In her very special case, it was truly the *person* who made the fashion.

If Dolley Madison wore it, no matter how old it was, no matter how many other fashions had come and gone, it could never be out of style. She had that much influence—even then!

$\mathcal{E}$LIZABETH $\mathcal{K}$ORTRIGHT $\mathcal{M}$ONROE

Born: June 30, 1768

Place of Birth: New York, NY

Parents: Capt. Lawrence Kortright, Hannah Aspinwall Kortright

Surviving Children: Eliza Kortright Monroe Hay; Maria Hester
Monroe Gouverneur

Marriage: February 16, 1786

First Lady: 1817-1825

Date of Death: September 23,1830

Burial Place: Hollywood Cemetery, Richmond VA

The Shadows
and The Rouge

For a woman who served eight full years as First Lady, Elizabeth Monroe is virtually overlooked and neglected.

Elizabeth Kortright's father had been a British officer during the French and Indian War. He decided to remain in the Colonies, married and made his home in New York. Little is documented of Elizabeth's upbringing, save that the family was comfortable, and she enjoyed all the amenities of growing up with a solid female education and privileges. She was a tiny woman, barely five feet tall, and in today's world, judging by one of her existing gowns, likely size two.

At eighteen she married James Monroe, ten years her senior and a foot taller. He had served with distinction as a Revolutionary War scout for General George Washington, and then read law with Virginia Governor Thomas Jefferson. He had been a delegate to the Virginia legislature and the Constitutional Convention. Suffice it to say that when he and Elizabeth married, Monroe was well-placed with excellent connections for the future. Finances, however, would always be spotty.

Shortly after their marriage, the Monroes were dispatched abroad by President George Washington, and the couple spent more than a decade in various diplomatic posts. Elizabeth's experiences in Paris, London and Madrid introduced her to a society far different from that in America, and it colored her outlook on the nuances of form and substance.

For a woman married to such a prominent Revolutionary War figure and diplomat, incredibly little is known about her. She seems to have made no real mark, and has left only a shadow of a trail. Part of that may be due to her predecessor Dolley Madison, larger than life. Or it could have been her distinct unpopularity as First Lady. It seems that the pomp of Europe served her poorly. Her fellow Americans thought she put on undemocratic airs.

James and Elizabeth Monroe had two daughters, born fifteen years apart. An infant son died, born somewhere between. If there had been a series of miscarriages along the way, which is certainly plausible, it was never recorded. Unlike the Adamses, who were genetically disposed to document everything, the Monroes were essentially private. Since they were together throughout most of their lives, few letters between them are available.

During their sojourn in Paris, Elizabeth witnessed both the Reign of Terror and the rise of Napoleon. Had she kept a diary, her recollections might have been fascinating, but none seems to exist. Their elder daughter, Eliza, was sent to a convent school, where she became close friends with the young Hortense Beauharnais, the daughter of Josephine, and thus stepdaughter to the Emperor Napoleon. Hortense later married Napoleon's brother and became Queen of the Netherlands. The friendship between the two former schoolmates would be lifelong, and the "imperial" connection made a serious impression on the distaff side of the Monroe family.

Elizabeth in France

Practically the only thing known about Elizabeth Monroe during her time in Paris was that *la belle Americaine,* as she was called (since she was considered very attractive), is sometimes credited with saving Madame Lafayette from the guillotine. Maybe.

The Marquis de Lafayette had become a great hero to the fledgling United States, and was truly beloved by President George Washington. That affection was returned with his whole Gallic heart; Lafayette's first born son would be named George Washington Lafayette, in honor of his godfather. The Marquis and James Monroe were the same age, and the two men had begun *their* lifelong friendship during the American Revolution. In the 1790s, during the Terror and its aftermath, Lafayette had been captured by the Austrians and imprisoned. Madame Lafayette had been sent to prison in Paris, sentenced to die on the guillotine for nothing more than her aristocratic connections.

Despite President Washington's deep personal concern for the Lafayette family, he needed to keep the new United States, only a few years old, free from political intrigue or apparent favoritism. With little clout in the world and more to lose than to gain, American orders to Minister Monroe were vague and cautious.

What *is* known, however, is that the American Minister made a public showing by sending *Mrs.* Monroe in a carriage, affixed with the seal of the United States, to visit Madame Lafayette in prison. The guards were likely astounded to see this tiny woman emerge, but no more than Mme. Lafayette. What conversation passed between the two ladies is unknown, but the next day, Mme. Lafayette was released and returned to her family.

The only other story credited to Elizabeth Monroe's sojourn in Europe is that she may have discovered cosmetics—commonplace on the continent. One version goes that she learned to use rouge discreetly and effectively, and perhaps was the one who introduced it to Dolley Madison back in the United States during the 1800s. Dolley was definitely known to *rouge*.

What is also interesting about Mrs. Monroe is that she appeared years younger than her true age. At least, that is what people said about her. When she was First Lady, she was in her late forties and already a grandmother. Most people thought she was ten years younger.

Maybe it was just the dim lighting.

An Important PS

While Elizabeth Monroe was surely one of the more obscure First Ladies, she has an equally obscure link to a true and important national treasure. Her great-granddaughter, Rose Gouverneur Hoes (1860-1933), had accumulated several of Elizabeth's personal belongings, as well as personal items from other First Ladies. In the early part of the twentieth century, Mrs. Hoes donated her collection to the Smithsonian Institution. This in turn became the nucleus for their famous and hugely popular collection of First Ladies' gowns and apparel.

The trail of history is always full of surprises.

Louisa Catherine Johnson Adams

Born: February 12, 1775

Place of Birth: London, England

Parents: Joshua Johnson; Catherine Nuth Johnson

Marriage: July 26, 1797

Surviving Children: George Washington Adams,

John Adams II, Charles Francis Adams

First Lady: 1825-1829

Date of Death: May 14, 1852

Burial Place: United First Parish Church, Quincy, MA

An *Inherited Veil*

*L*ouisa Catherine Johnson Adams was half-American. Her father was Maryland-born, but he had lived in England since early manhood. There he had prospered, married, and raised a family. London-born and Paris-educated, Louisa was raised from birth to be exactly what she would become—the wife of an important diplomat and player on the world stage. She was a pretty girl-to-woman, well-educated, talented, trained to charm and grace parlor and table.

Her engagement and subsequent marriage to John Quincy Adams in 1797 was a definite coup for the Johnson family. JQA, as he usually referred to himself, was a rising young diplomat, and the son of the Vice President of the United States. Unfortunately, when the young Adamses returned to America, her New England in-laws were aloof.

Although John Adams Sr. would grow very fond of his English-born daughter-in-law, and she would learn to love him dearly, Louisa never had a close relationship with her formidable mother-in-law. Abigail had been disdainful toward her brilliant son's non-brilliant marriage, believing that the pampered Englishwoman would not be tough enough.

Nevertheless, Abigail obviously bequeathed her *poet's veil* to her charming but not-very-resilient daughter-in-law. It is, of course, the veil shielding deep and private feelings, never to be shared outside of family, perhaps never completely shared with anyone. If those feelings are known at all, they must be inferred by osmosis and even then, left unsaid. Louisa, like all early Adamses, including spouses, was a regular diarist and correspondent. While most of her letters are discreet and cautious, her diaries occasionally lift the veil to her heart and soul.

Louisa Catherine Adams had a long history as a generally unhappy and neglected wife. All indications are that the cranky and extremely controlling John Quincy truly loved his graceful consort, but he seldom expressed it. Nor did he extend the regard and respect that his own parents had demonstrated toward each other so freely. Louisa was mostly relegated to woman-stuff—ornament and mother—except when her husband needed her abundant social charms. (JQA had mega diplomatic skill, but was nil in the social department.)

JQA himself was never a teetotaler, and in fact, could even be considered a heavy drinker. Having spent his formative years in the great capitals of Europe, he was introduced early, as most Europeans are, to the fruits of the vine. But John Quincy Adams was never an alcoholic. Perhaps the traits that caused addiction in his brothers Charles and Thomas had managed to escape him.

But like his parents, JQA and his wife, Louisa, had three sons who lived to maturity. Two would fall under the old Smith-Adams curse. Only their third son, named for his hapless Uncle Charles, rose to meet their great expectations.

The beginning of the eventual failings of George Washington Adams and his brother John Adams II might be traced to their father's appointment as Minister Plenipotentiary to St. Petersburg, Russia by President James Madison in 1809. Over Louisa's bitter tears and anxieties, Mr. and Mrs. JQA left their older sons, then eleven and nine, with family members in Massachusetts. They would not see their older boys again for five years. By that time they were half-grown men their parents barely recognized.

When George and John were finally sent for, the happy family reunion was shadowed by the Puritanical bloodline that ran strong in the Adams family, and particularly cold and harsh in

JQA. His powerful ambition combined with unrelenting purpose and discipline, and he expected no less from his sons. When they rebelled against the moral lectures and hour-by-hour schedules he created for them, the demanding father merely tightened the tether. Louisa was powerless against her husband's controlling disposition. The young men grew more and more discouraged.

When the family returned to America, they went to Harvard, and duly became lawyers—against their own inclinations and talents.

Uncle Charles' Nephew

George Washington Adams, named for the country's first president, was a sensitive, poetic fellow, more like his mother than his father. He was handsome, charming and ripe for falling in love with Louisa's niece, Mary Hellen, a flirtatious young woman who made her home with Aunt and Uncle Adams in Washington when her parents died. They agreed to marry. But when George returned to Massachusetts to make another half-hearted attempt at lawyering, he became "out of sight, out of mind" for the fickle Mary. George's younger brother John was equally handsome—and available. He caught Mary's eye, and she married *him* instead. George was now a failure in romance as well as in his profession, and particularly in his father's eyes. The same demons that had afflicted the Uncle Charles he had never known took hold of George with the same intensity and results. His drinking, his inertia and his need for the human affection he could never find became a freefall.

As JQA was about to retire as President in 1829, he sent for his wayward oldest son. George dutifully booked passage on a steamship to Washington. Perhaps unable to face more of his father's certain disapproval, and perhaps realizing that his life had become a desperate unending abyss, he slipped over the railing and was never seen again. He was only twenty-eight.

Louisa's veil, the veil to conceal her pain, her loss, her disappointment and perhaps her own feelings of helplessness, would shroud her soul. For the rest of her life, she insisted George's death was an accident. Others knew better. Perhaps she knew it, too.

Uncle Tom's Nephew

If George Adams resembled his Uncle Charles, John Adams II seemed to follow in the footsteps of his Uncle Thomas, more or less a controlled alcoholic.

When JQA was elected President, his middle son became his secretary. Mary Hellen, his capricious young ward, went with them to the White House. There, a romance blossomed between her and John, her fiancé's brother, much to the dismay of the First Lady, who feared sorrowful repercussions.

The situation finally progressed to a point of urgent need of clerical blessing. At Louisa's insistence, John and Mary married in the White House—the only president's son to do so. It was a small wedding. Neither George nor Charles Francis attended.

Alas for John II, however. His professional efforts failed, both in law and in business. Alcohol took its toll as it had with his Uncle Thomas. John died of its complications at only thirty-one. He left two daughters.

It is been suggested that shared grief over the early and unfortunate deaths of their two older sons became a catalyst to bring the long-strained relationship between Mr. and Mrs. JQA to a better place. The little granddaughters had a happy effect on Grandpa JQ's disposition. If sons (and presumably grandsons) were to be disciplined, little girls were to be pampered and petted. John and Louisa Adams' later years are usually considered their marital best; certainly their happiest.

Whatever unhappiness or insecurity or lack of value Louisa may have felt was expressed only to her diary. Her metaphorical poet's veil remained intact, shrouding, clouding and concealing so many of her private despairs. Years later, when their youngest son Charles Francis edited his grandmother Abigail's papers for publication, he asked his aging mother to assist him. In reading those long-ago letters and diaries, Louisa remarked, "I wish I had known her better." They might have had much more in common than they thought.

Louisa's Non-Gown Story

*A*s a rising young diplomat and the son of the Vice President of the United States, John Quincy Adams was a great catch for anyone. As the daughter of a wealthy Maryland merchant who had emigrated to London before the American Revolution, Louisa Catherine Johnson had been well educated and schooled in all the social graces befitting a woman of her stature. On their wedding day in 1797, however, Joshua Johnson, the bride's father, confided to the groom that he had incurred serious business reverses. If young Adams expected a munificent dowry to relieve him of the petty concerns of finance, it would not be forthcoming. Indeed, the entire Johnson family would return to the United States to spend the rest of their lives in low-level government positions, courtesy of Adams connections.

Like his parents, JQA was financially comfortable, but hardly wealthy. He would never be wealthy.

The Adamses in Russia

In 1809, forty-one-year-old John Quincy Adams was appointed by President James Madison to be Minister

Plenipotentiary to the court of Tsar Alexander, in St. Petersburg, Russia. It was considered one of the most important diplomatic posts on the continent. Louisa went in a sea of tears because her stern husband had made all the arrangements, and had insisted that their sons George and John, ages eleven and nine, remain with family to be educated in Massachusetts. Only Charles Francis would go with them to Europe. He was still a baby, not even fully weaned. It was a wrenching experience for Louisa, and colored the five years of her sojourn in Russia, and perhaps the rest of her life.

The Tsarist court of the Napoleonic years was a mishmash of opulence and glitter mixed with the primitive and crude manners of its medieval serfdom, still pervasive. Fortunately, the Tsar liked and admired the American diplomat, and extended many courtesies and preferences. But medieval or not, court manners demand strict adherence. They are inviolate, and in an absolute monarchy like Russia, where great importance is placed on form, all who attend royal functions are expected to obey their customs to the letter.

John Quincy Adams had no personal wealth to draw upon. His salary, munificent by American standards of the early 1800s, may have been second only to that of the President, but it was still insufficient for maintaining the style expected in high Russian court circles. His European diplomatic counterparts were of the nobility, with deep, deep pockets.

To complicate the situation, communication between the United States and Russia took an ocean voyage of several weeks, plus a long overland journey, with the potential for many mishaps along the way, courtesy of the Napoleonic Wars. Letters, and more importantly, John's salary checks, were sporadic at best. The Adamses needed to maintain a strict budget; debt was abhorrent to them.

Court dress was—and in some countries still is—a major part of court etiquette. Immaculate care was given to the cut of a man's jacket, the length of his trousers or breeches, the condition of his kid gloves, and assorted other matters that seem trivial today. It was vitally important then. Ladies, of course, required the most fashionable and expensive gowns, jewelry, dancing slippers, fans, furs and other adornments. If the men dressed for success, the ladies dressed to impress.

Louisa Adams had been considered one of the most fashionable and well-dressed women in Washington, but Washington was not St. Petersburg. At least on one documented occasion, regrets were sent to the Tsar, claiming her ubiquitous "unwellness," and John Quincy went unescorted to the ball. The truth this time? Mrs. Adams' formal silver tissue ball gown, the only one she had expressly suitable for court appearances, had been seen by everyone—perhaps several times. She already had reworked it with lace or trim and by altering sleeves and necklines. So this time and for this occasion, an elegant new gown was absolutely imperative for the occasion.

The Adamses simply could not afford it.

The *W*arm *C*loak

*L*ouisa Adams' cloak story is both a legitimate article of clothing and its own metaphor. As the wife of the Minister Plentipotentiary to the Tsar of Russia, Louisa Catherine Adams spent nearly five years in St. Petersburg, where winters are legendary. Of *course* she had a warm cloak, most likely some kind of fur. She likely had more than one, and very probably fur blankets as well. They were a necessity, not a luxury.

In 1814, as the second American war with Great Britain was going nowhere except to a negotiated truce, John Quincy Adams, senior diplomat on the continent, was designated to lead the negotiations in Ghent (the Netherlands). He departed Russia hastily, leaving his wife and their six-year-old son. Some months later, he sent the following instructions, to wit: pack what you need, purchase what you need, sell what you don't need, and meet me in Paris.

At nearly forty, about the same age her mother-in-law Abigail had been when she traveled alone to Europe to meet her husband, Louisa Catherine Adams had been a protected wife, dominated and generally neglected by her brilliant but overbearing husband. She now faced more responsibility than ever before, with little experience or disposition for the hardships she would encounter.

Nevertheless, she diligently followed her husband's instructions. She sold their furnishings and unnecessary possessions. She purchased the best carriage in St. Petersburg, which was poorly made and inadequate at best, engaged a driver and only two servants to accompany them, and packed their belongings. She may have even paid a final visit to the tiny grave of their last child, a baby daughter, who was born, died and is forever buried on Russian soil. Louisa said her formal goodbyes, and set out in mid-winter, over a six-hundred-mile trek across northern Europe. She resolved to make her stern husband proud of her resourcefulness, and relied on her language skills: some Russian, passable German, fluent French—the language of nearly all Europeans—and of course, English.

The journey took six weeks over mud-rutted roads—when there *were* roads—across what today is Estonia, northern Poland, northern Germany which then was divided into its various city states, and finally northern France.

The trip was plotted from village to village, town to town, in the hope that some lodging, a fireplace, fresh horses and a warm bed and supper could be obtained. Louisa hoped for a semblance of diplomatic courtesy, once the locals recognized her prominence as an *American* diplomat's wife.

Her carriage broke down with alarming regularity. The driver, the local guides and servants were unreliable and dishonest. Then there was the weather in northern Europe, horrible that time of year: freezing cold, followed by unexpected thaw and mud and rain. Then more rain and snow. There were times when even the comfort of a small tavern could not be found, and Louisa's warm cloak and fur blankets literally became their refuge as she hugged her child tight as they slept in their carriage seats, listening to the howling wind—or maybe wolves echoing in the nearby forests.

If that fear and discomfort were not enough strain on the determination and stamina of a woman whose background was schooled for banquets and ballrooms, she learned that the recently deposed Napoleon Bonaparte had just escaped from Elba, his island of exile, and was reforming his army. Wherever

Louisa went, ragtag soldiers were once again amassing to fight either for or against the now undeposed Emperor. A woman of obvious quality traveling in a Russian-made carriage with only a small child and two servants was immediately suspect. Her flawless French was now her biggest asset, along with two decades of diplomatic charm skills.

At one point, soldiers wearing the Emperor's colors threatened to overturn her carriage. She put her little boy's soldier-hat on her own head and waved his toy sword in the air, crying, *"Vive la France! Vive la Empereur!"* They let her pass unmolested.

It was a harrowing ordeal, and perhaps Louisa's finest hour. *She* was in charge of her own life and the life of her young son. *She* was the one who directed the course and made the decisions. *She* was the one whose fears needed to be firmly kept in check. *She* was the one to whom the servants and her son looked to for leadership. She had never been a leader, other than of fashionable society.

The Metaphorical Cloak

Perhaps the worst part of this great adventure was the metaphorical cloak. Louisa had no audience to bear witness to her composure, to her courage, to her inner strength, to her resourcefulness, to her surprising leadership, and even to the event itself. The servants and guides were discharged and disappeared. Her son was too young to have any more than a small boy's scattered memories. The cloak that had warmed her in reality provided no warmth of appreciation. When John Quincy Adams met her in Paris, he was astonished by her tale. He had expected it to be a reasonably routine journey.

A decade later, Louisa Adams was First Lady, living in the White House. Her always-delicate health had deteriorated and she was menopausal as well. Family woes added to her plate of cares. Her cranky husband, unpopular and constantly thwarted, was crankier than ever. What should have been the pinnacle of success and glory was a morass of gloom and depression all around.

Sometime later, seeking solace for her own losses and disappointments, Louisa wrote a little play based upon her adventures between St. Petersburg and Paris in the middle of winter and in the middle of war-torn Napoleonic Europe. The metaphorical *warm cloak* failed once again, and provided no warmth. Her little play was never read nor produced on any stage. No one even knew she wrote it. She called it *The Adventures of A Nobody*, and put it away for the centuries.

RACHEL DONELSON ROBARDS JACKSON

Born: June 15 (?), 1767

Place of Birth: Halifax County, VA

Parents: Col. John Donelson; Rachel Stockley Donelson

Marriage: Lewis Robards (1), 1785 (div.) - No children

Andrew Jackson (2) August, 1791;

reaffirmed January 17, 1794

No children of either marriage

First Lady: Did not serve (died shortly before

Jackson's inauguration)

Date of Death: December 22, 1828

Burial Place: The Hermitage, Nashville, TN

$\mathcal{I}$naugural $\mathcal{G}$own

$\mathcal{T}$he Smithsonian Institution maintains a priceless collection of First Ladies' inaugural gowns—at least, those of the past hundred years. Had they collected and maintained *all* First Lady inaugural gowns, the most expensive could arguably be the one purchased by Rachel Donelson Jackson for her husband's inauguration on March 4, 1829.

When Andrew Jackson was elected in 1828, both Jacksons were sixty-one years old and in poor health. He had a long list of chronic ailments, although he lived to be seventy-eight. She, on the other hand, had a bad heart, or dropsy, as they called it then.

The Jacksons had been a loving and devoted couple, married nearly forty years, but their marriage was marred by scandal and slander spawned by the murky details of her unhappy first marriage; she had been, of all horrors, a divorcée. Her reputation was further sullied by the fact that her marriage to Jackson had come before her divorce was legally finalized. Jackson fought duels to defend her reputation, and carried two bullets in his body for decades.

Then there were long separations due to Jackson's prominence, his politics and his outsized personality. Rachel's comfort came in the seclusion of their well-named Hermitage plantation in Nashville, Tennessee, surrounded by her many siblings and their families. She became reclusive, heightened further by her growing religious fanaticism.

Her social manners, while acceptable in frontier Tennessee where her family was well known, were unacceptable in the polite societies of cosmopolitan cities. Her education was spotty at best. Her conversation was limited. In short, she was ill-suited to wear the mantle of the quintessential Dolley Madison—or the sophisticated and cultured Elizabeth Monroe and Louisa Adams. To make matters worse, Rachel had grown very stout.

Despite her misgivings and personal disinclination, she agreed to go to Washington with her newly-elected husband because she knew he wanted her near, and as always, she wanted to please him. She invited two nieces along to do the socializing. She would plead her ill-health and remain secluded, and even wrote to a friend that she would rather "be a doorkeeper in the house of the Lord than to live in that great white palace."

Still, Rachel needed to make an appearance in Washington, and an appropriate gown was needed for the Inaugural. She went to a dressmaker in Nashville. Some modern historians claim she was poorly guided by her friends, and perhaps the dressmaker: the gown she selected was white and more suitable to a young bride than a heavy, dropsical woman past sixty. We will never know for sure.

A short time later, Rachel went for a fitting and saw a newspaper story rehashing her unhappy first marriage, her scandalous divorce and subsequent bigamous remarriage. Even though the Jacksons had immediately remarried when they learned the facts, the scandal had wings and a long life. If roiling those muddy waters wasn't enough to cause Rachel pain, the article commented that Mrs. Jackson was unfit for her new role, and that she would bring disgrace to the White House.

Rachel left the shop in hysterics. Her friends brought her back to the Hermitage where she suffered a heart attack a few days later. She died on December 22, 1828. Andrew Jackson insisted to his dying day that she was killed by calumny, and that those who slandered her must look to God for forgiveness, since he would never forgive them himself. Ten weeks later, a grieving

Jackson took his oath of office wearing a mourning band.

Rachel was buried in her beloved Hermitage flower garden, wearing that same white gown she planned to wear the evening of March 4, 1829. It was a gown no one would ever see.

It is arguably the most expensive inaugural gown in First Lady history. It cost Rachel Jackson her life.

Julia Gardiner Tyler

Born: May 4, 1820

Place of Birth: Gardiner's Island, NY

Parents: State Senator David Gardiner;

Juliana McLachlen Gardiner

Marriage: June 26, 1844*

Surviving Children: David Gardiner Tyler, John Alexander Tyler,

Julia Tyler Spencer, Lachlan Tyler, Lyon Gardiner Tyler, Robert

Fitzwalter Tyler, Pearl Tyler Ellis

First Lady: 1844-1845

Date of Death: July 10, 1889

Burial Place: Hollywood Cemetery, Richmond, VA

*Julia Tyler was the second wife of John Tyler.
His first wife, Letitia Christian, was crippled by a stroke
and died in the White House after thirty years of marriage.

Miss G's Shopping Bag

*N*ineteen-year-old Julia Gardiner was an extremely wealthy New York socialite. Her state senator father, David Gardiner, was one of the richest men on Long Island; her mother, the only child of a successful and even wealthier brewer. Julia attended the best private finishing school for young ladies, had the most elegant wardrobe, the most fashionable carriage at her disposal, and spent her free time in Saratoga Springs, the emerging playground of the rich.

Somehow—and this is where the story gets dicey—the New York merchants Bogert and Mecamly obtained an etching of pretty Miss Gardiner, which they proceeded to use for their advertising purposes. Early biographers left it at the "somehow-they-obtained" stage. Modern historians seem to concur that Julia Gardiner herself must have been complicit in the acquisition. It makes sense. After all, in the late 1830s photography was still unknown, although etchings and other print forms had been around for centuries. Julia's etched likeness may have been commissioned by her wealthy family, but it would never have been a commodity. It would have been reserved strictly for family purposes. But at only nineteen, Miss Gardiner may have been seduced by the inference that she was pretty, popular and worth the merchants' interest, and that the Messrs. Bogert and Mecamly might reciprocate with the latest ribbons and fans and dress goods. It is a thought.

Whatever the motives or mechanisms, the upshot was that the merchants disseminated handbills advertising their wares. The handbill depicted a young society demoiselle holding a large shopping bag on which was printed: "I'll purchase at Bogert and Mecamly's, No. 86 Ninth Avenue. Their Goods are Beautiful and Astonishingly Cheap." Not that Julia cared about price tags. The flyer identified the young lady as "Miss Julia Gardiner, the Rose of Long Island."

The handbills raised eyebrows, particularly those of Julia's parents. A week or two later a Brooklyn newspaper printed an anonymous love poem dedicated to "The Rose of Long Island." It was now the stuff of scandals. This was an age when no respectable lady permitted her name to appear in the newspapers, let alone in an advertisement for merchandise!

Julia may well have enjoyed the flurry of attention, but the State Senator and Mrs. Gardiner took a very dim view of the affair, especially since they took a very serious view of their position in society. Without further ado, they packed up the family and whisked themselves off for a two-year Grand Tour of Europe, to let the talk die down.

Julia Gardiner's fling as a merchant's spokeswoman made little if any impact on history, although some claim she was the first person used to promote another's wares. Maybe. Within five years, however, she managed to generate the interest of John Tyler, the widowed President of the United States, and before long, "The Rose of Long Island" would have a new soubriquet: First Lady of the Land.

$\mathcal{S}$ARAH $\mathcal{C}$HILDRESS $\mathcal{P}$OLK

Date of Birth: September 4, 1803

Place of Birth: Murfreesboro, TN

Parents: Capt. Joel Childress; Elizabeth Whitsitt Childress

Marriage: January 1, 1824; no children

First Lady: 1845-1849

Date of Death: August 14, 1891

Burial Place: Tennessee State Capitol, Nashville, TN

$\mathcal{F}$ans

$\mathcal{S}$arah Childress was a Tennessee woman, intelligent and devout. Her excellent education at a Moravian finishing school was cut short by the untimely death of her father.

At twenty, she married Tennessee lawyer-with-ambition James Knox Polk. Legend says that it was the great Andrew Jackson who suggested that the young politician "look no farther" than Miss Childress when choosing a wife. If so, it proved to be good advice. The marriage was a happy union.

Partly because of her innate intelligence, partly because of her religious upbringing, partly because of the political discussion that was part of the Childress daily dinner table routine, and perhaps mostly because the Polk marriage was childless, Sarah became a close companion to her politician husband. Few letters exist between them, since they were seldom apart for very long with little need to correspond.

With no family responsibilities at home, little inclination to domesticity, health unimpaired by childbirth, and their two plantations satisfactorily maintained by overseers, she was free to accompany her congressman husband to Washington. She was popular among the congressional social set. The women liked her. So did their husbands.

Sarah the Fashionista

Sarah was a good-looking woman by all accounts. She was not tall. Polk himself was one of the shorter presidents, perhaps five-foot-seven. But she was well-figured and had intelligent eyes. She wore her dark hair in fashionable corkscrew curls, sometimes adorned with feather plumes or other stylish accents. She favored jewel-toned deep colors, like royal blue or rich maroon or emerald green, which accented her dark complexion.

The low-cut Empire gowns popularized in America by Dolley Madison had long been out of style by the mid-1840s when Sarah was First Lady and in her prime. Women of that era were more reserved. Necklines were generally higher; sleeves were long, certainly in the daytime. While Sarah was considered impeccably attired, her fashion taste was modest, even in a modest age. She displayed nothing of the overtly fashionable image of Julia Tyler, her young predecessor, seventeen years her junior. The few portraits and photographs of Mrs. Polk depict a well-dressed woman, but far from flashy. The devout Presbyterian was a serious-minded lady.

First Lady Sarah Polk was always admired by her peers, male and female, for her decorous manners, her intelligence, her industry and her thrift. To save salary money during the Polk administration, she personally assumed the President's secretarial duties. She filed his papers, copied his correspondence in her firm hand, kept the appointment book, and scoured dozens of newspapers for articles that might be of interest to him. While the Polks were pleasant and generally sociable, frivolity was not tolerated. They came to Washington to work.

Fans

Perhaps the most important accessory for a nineteenth-century woman was her fan. Jewelry was a luxury. A head covering was an age-old tradition. A lady's fan, however, was a necessity, particularly amongst women of that certain age when great changes occur.

There was no air conditioning nor any table-mounted electric fans. Clothing was designed to cover, especially women's clothing, with its hoops and petticoats and yards and yards of material. It was hot, pure and simple.

In their teens, young ladies may have been taught to use the unspoken language of fans for many reasons: flirtatious coquetry, modesty, and fashion statements, but essentially a fan was used for its stated purpose: to create a breeze.

The basic style of a fan never varied. Most ladies' fan frames were made from ivory or bone, and sometimes wood. Then the ribs were covered with various fabrics or specialty papers, decorated in any number of ways. Most women had several fans in their wardrobe, and being well-to-do as well as a high-ranking congressional wife—Polk was Speaker of the House of Representatives for a time—Sarah no doubt had many. She had them for daytime wear, for casual veranda-sitting, and for evening or formal occasions. All were designed to coordinate with her gowns.

One of her documented—and existing—fans is made of a delicate white lace, which naturally went with everything.

Perhaps her most renowned fan is the one she was given by her husband at the time of his inauguration as president in 1845. It was a magnificent object of silk and ivory, with portraits of all Polk's predecessors hand-painted in the folds. It was one-of-a-kind, and remains today as one of the treasures at a Polk family home in Columbia, Tennessee. (Polk Place, their primary home in Nashville, was destroyed by fire long ago.)

The Metaphorical Fan

Polk retired from his single term in 1849 and died only three months later, many claim from overwork. Sarah was only forty-four. She would be a professional widow for more than four decades. Her fans now took on a metaphorical purpose: they allowed her to hide within public sight, which she believed was her womanly duty. It is said she seldom left her house in Nashville except to go to church.

The Victorian age had settled in solidly by mid-nineteenth century, and the prompt remarriage tradition of an earlier era was replaced by long, if not eternal, mourning. Like Mary Lincoln, Lucretia Garfield and Ida McKinley, widowed First Ladies who followed her, Sarah wore nothing but black thereafter.

She busied herself with some good works, hosting occasional parties for orphaned children, and enjoying weekly tea-visits from her minister. But mostly she sorted and organized her husband's papers. Her reputation and pious reserve kept Polk Place off-limits for both Union and Confederate soldiers, who otherwise used most of Tennessee as a battlefield. Visiting dignitaries to Nashville always made a point of paying their respects to the former First Lady. She herself made no political statements, and only released her slaves when it became law.

Whatever talents or intelligence Sarah had, whatever opinions or political philosophies she espoused or decried, and whatever opportunities she may have let slip away were forever hidden by her metaphorical fan. It kept her away from the public's prying eye.

Perhaps it also hid her yawn of self-inflicted boredom.

JANE MEANS APPLETON PIERCE

Born: March 12, 1806

Place of Birth: Hampton, NH

Parents: Rev. Jesse Appleton, Elizabeth Means Appleton

Marriage: November 10, 1834

Children: 2 d. early childhood; Benjamin, d. age 11

First Lady: 1853-57

Died: December 2, 1863

Place of Burial: Old North Cemetery, Concord, NH

Handkerchiefs

Facial tissues are a twentieth century invention. In fact, well into the mid-twentieth century, most women still favored the old fashioned handkerchief.

Hankies come in dozens of styles, colors and fabrics—cotton, lace, linen, silk and many other materials. They are easily washed, dried and ironed. They were frequently embroidered, trimmed and monogrammed. Prices ranged from the sublime to the ridiculous. They were hugely appropriate for a gentleman to give to a lady-friend. All women, regardless of status, had them and no *lady* would venture out without a freshly laundered hankie in her purse.

Handkerchiefs served several purposes, of course: catching the occasional sneeze, deflecting a cough, dabbing a slightly runny nose, wiping a speck of dust away, or dealing with the facial damps of children. Hankies also had social uses—giving to favored beaux for remembrance, casually dropping it to attract the attention of a potential beau, or waving it from a window as the beau passed by, either for encouragement or farewell.

Then of course, there were tears.

The Jane Story

Jane Appleton Pierce was a New England woman, after whose name the words *joy* or *pleasure* would seldom follow in a sentence. She was a dour woman, perhaps possessed of a sorrowful gene from birth. A genetic disposition toward depression is not unknown. Jane's father, a Congregationalist minister-educator, appears to have been similarly inclined. It is said that his religious fervor induced him to starve himself to death by excessive fasting.

Jane Appleton was a frail child, perhaps tubercular. Between her delicate health, her morbidly religious upbringing, which acknowledged a punishing God, and whatever genetic tendencies she could not help, Jane required a small-world life. She did not get it. And try as she did to crawl back into her sheltered mouse-hole, life drew her into a larger venue and a mismatched union.

Franklin Pierce was a convivial man by nature. Jane was reticent. He enjoyed camaraderie; she preferred a small circle of mostly relatives. He gravitated heartily to politics and the grand stage. She withdrew, horrified by its ungodliness.

Franklin Pierce did not marry until he was nearly thirty-two. Jane was twenty-eight, considered an old maid by that time. When they did marry, Pierce had already embarked on his Congressional career. They honeymooned in Washington where the new bride was miserable. Her handkerchiefs came in handy, due to the sniffles and coughs from the capital's well-known abysmal climate. There were also tears. Jane disliked socializing in general, but in particular with those she believed were too worldly for her sense of morality. She seldom left her rooms except to attend church.

Subsequent Congressional sessions saw Franklin Pierce going to Washington alone.

Jane Pierce, Mother

Jane became pregnant soon after her marriage, and was elated at the birth of their first son. To her, motherhood was the supreme function of women, and the *raison d'etre* in her life.

Many handkerchiefs were needed, since the baby was sickly and died only months after his birth.

The birth of their second son, Frank, rejuvenated the chronically melancholy mother, aided by Pierce's promise to forswear politics, at least on a national level, and to forswear alcohol, both of which were high on his list of pleasures. Pierce appears to have truly loved his "Jeanie" and sincerely tried in both efforts. He declined an appointment as Attorney General in James Polk's cabinet. He even became the president of the Concord, New Hampshire Temperance Society. But he would fail to reform permanently in either case.

The couple's third son, Bennie, born when Jane was thirty-eight, was her last chance at motherhood. Then little Frank died at only four years old, and Bennie became the heart, soul and life of Jane Pierce.

For a few years, she was as close to being happy as she would ever be. She had a son to dote upon, and a husband who remained both sober and at home. She enjoyed her regular visits from their minister. She was content to spend an evening sewing and listening to Bennie recite his Sunday School lessons.

The FLOTUS-to-be

By 1852, sectionalism and the spread of slavery had begun to drive ominous wedges into the political fabric, to a point of national paralysis. The Democrats had few leaders who were acceptable to the entire country. Pierce, of course, was aware of this dilemma, and realized that his view on slavery won him Southern friends. While he did not favor the institution, he believed it was protected by the Constitution. Being a New Englander and a non-slave owner made him acceptable in the North. He quietly encouraged interest in his nomination, all the while assuring his reluctant wife that he had been away from the national scene too long for anyone to remember him. They remembered.

After an exhausting forty-nine ballots, the Democrats nominated Franklin Pierce, the Northerner-with-Southern-sympathy, as their presidential candidate. The story goes that when Jane heard the news, she fainted dead away, thus providing yet another handkerchief usage— doused with smelling salts to revive the swoon.

After much soul-searching, Jane determined that Pierce's nomination and subsequent election must be God's will. She made a feeble effort to accept the inevitable, and invited a childhood friend who had married into her family to help with the traditional First Lady social duties that were abhorrent to her.

The Tragedy of Jane

Only a few weeks before the Pierces were to leave for Washington, they went to visit family members in Massachusetts. En route their train derailed, and little Bennie was caught between the cars and crushed to death. It was an overwhelming shock to his mother, and she would never recover from the trauma.

Searching her soul even deeper, trying to find divine reason for the freak accident, she finally determined that God took Bennie to punish them for leaving home. Then she thought longer, and concluded that perhaps it was so the child wouldn't be a distraction to his President father. Either way, it was a mammoth guilt-trip laid on Franklin Pierce, the poor grieving father.

The journey to Washington was sad for both mourning parents. Then came the final and unforgiveable blow. Jane inadvertently learned that Pierce had misled her (blatantly lied) by suggesting that he had not desired nor encouraged the nomination. Jane Pierce had lost her son and now lost faith in her husband's word.

Jane left the train when it stopped in Baltimore, unable to continue. She remained there for several weeks, too distraught to attend the sober inaugural. If she ever truly forgave her husband for his deception, it is unknown.

She remained mostly secluded in the White House during Pierce's entire administration, allowing her relative-by-marriage to assume the modest social duties. It is said that the First Lady spent a good part of her time writing letters to her dead son, begging his forgiveness and intercession with the hereafter on behalf of his poor grief-stricken mother.

No doubt she dabbed away many a tear on her handkerchief.

$\mathcal{H}$ARRIET $\mathcal{L}$ANE $\mathcal{J}$OHNSTON

Born: May 9, 1830

Place of Birth: Mecklensburg, PA

Parents: Elliott Tole Lane and Jane Buchanan Lane

Marriage: January 11, 1866, to Henry Elliott Johnston

Children: 2 sons, d. early

Presidential Hostess: 1857-1861

Died: July 3, 1903

Place of Burial: Green Mount Cemetery, Baltimore, MD

An Open Purse

Harriet Lane is seldom considered in the pantheon of First Ladies, probably for two reasons: First, James Buchanan, the fifteenth President, was a generally ineffectual man, who despite a creditable resume of government service, was ill-equipped to deal with the turmoil preceding the Civil War. The second reason is that despite the genuine elegance of Washington society between 1857 and 1861 when Harriet Lane occupied the White House, she was niece-of, rather than wife-of President Buchanan.

Harriet Lane was orphaned at nine years old. Her bachelor Uncle James Buchanan, already a well-established Pennsylvania attorney and Congressman of rising stature, became her legal guardian, dedicated to raising her in a manner befitting his prominent station in life. She was sent to the best finishing schools, provided with the finest clothing and accouterments, and most of all, the sincere love and affection of a benevolent uncle. He could not have been more devoted had he been her own father.

In turn, Harriet grew up to be brighter than most, pretty, accomplished, and dedicated to her uncle. At eighteen, she mingled with Washington's elite. At twenty-two, she was the lovely young lady on Buchanan's arm while he was U.S. Minister to Great Britain. Her charm and poise won the admiration of all, including Queen Victoria and Prince Albert, who were said to be persnickety in that department.

So in 1856, when Buchanan was elected President, Harriet had already become an accomplished leader of whatever society she entered, thus a fitting "acting-First Lady" or hostess for the Chief Executive.

The four years of Buchanan's presidency may have been unpopular, but Harriet's governance of Washington society glittered. She was young and pretty, stylish without being flashy, and personable. Washingtonians liked her. Her social prominence culminated in the grand event they hosted for Albert Edward, the young Prince of Wales, and the first of British royalty to visit its erstwhile colonies.

One might conjecture that had Harriet Lane been *Mrs.* James Buchanan rather than merely his niece, she would have ranked highly among her sisterhood. She was a woman of substantive interests and accomplishments. But she was not Mrs. B., and once the Buchanan administration had ended, Miss Lane retired to the Buchanan oblivion.

The Later Years

Harriet Lane waited until she was thirty-five before she married. She had fair looks, charm and position, and numerous beaux. If she waited, it was her own choice, and that choice was Henry E. Johnston, a well-regarded and very wealthy Baltimore attorney and businessman.

By this time, James Buchanan was well past seventy and in failing health. He was delighted with the match, knowing that his dear niece would be taken care of. He could die in peace, which he did a year after their wedding. Harriet was his major heir.

She went on to have two sons, James and Henry, but her years as a happy matron were short lived. Both her sons died in their early teens from rheumatic fever. Her husband died not long thereafter. Mrs. Johnston became a very wealthy widow.

As an aside, there have been several wealthy widows among our First Ladies, and if not wealthy per se, certainly nicely fixed. Harriet Lane Johnston stands uniquely. Despite serving for four full years as a quasi-First Lady, she was not a presidential widow, and thus ineligible for the widow's pension that was instituted in the mid-1870s. She also did not need the money.

When Harriet became a widow at fifty-four, she had no heirs. Her uncle was gone. Her sons had died. Her husband had died. She had outlived her siblings. She was alone. Her personal needs were minimal and she could live very comfortably, which she did, without making a dent in all that she had inherited. What should she do? What would be *her* legacy?

Harriet's Purse

Harriet Lane Johnston had a great deal of money to disburse, and well before her life drew close to its end in 1903 she began to direct its disposal.

First and foremost, she endowed a modern equivalent of $2 million to create a free pediatric medical center at the new (1893) Johns Hopkins School of Medicine in Baltimore, Maryland. It would be named the Harriet Lane Home, and was the first medical facility exclusively dedicated to research and treatment for the diseases of children. This would be her lasting legacy to the memory of her two sons who had died so young.

Harriet had also been an avid art collector ever since her youthful days in London, when she began to acquire several classical oil paintings. During Buchanan's presidential years, she generously invited artists to White House receptions and personally introduced them to potential patrons. She had a long-term dream of seeing an American Gallery of Art to rival those in Europe. At her death, she bequeathed her personal collection to the Smithsonian Institution, where it became the nucleus for what today is the National Gallery of Art.

Harriet had been born into a Presbyterian family but joined the Episcopal Church when she married. When the Washington Cathedral was chartered in the 1890s, she took an active interest in it. Inspired by the Vienna Boys Choir on a trip to Austria, she envisioned its counterpart in America. Training and supporting a boys choir would naturally require funds, and Mrs. Johnston was happy to underwrite the Saint Alban's School, including generous endowments for scholarships.

Finally, Harriet Lane Johnston had been sincerely devoted to her benevolent uncle, and it must have been painful for her to see his reputation falter so badly after a lifetime of high achievement. She left more than $100,000 to erect a monument in Washington to the memory of our Fifteenth President.

There was no big hoopla when her will was read.

Harriet's Legacy Today

Harriet Lane Johnston took great pains making her will with its many provisions. Everything was well considered and planned. The interesting part is that every major bequest—the Johns Hopkins pediatric medical center, the National Gallery of Art, the Saint Alban's School, and the monument to James Buchanan—are still around after more than a century.

Her influence as a not-quite-First Lady, merely niece-of President, may have consigned Harriet Lane to a minor role in history, but her generosity, her foresight and the substance of her very sizeable bequests do her great, great honor.

Mary Ann Todd Lincoln

Born: December 13, 1818

Place of Birth: Lexington, KY

Parents: Robert Smith Todd; Eliza Ann Parker Todd

Marriage: November 4, 1842

Children: Robert Todd Lincoln, Edward Baker Lincoln (d. age 3);

William Wallace Lincoln (d. age 11); Thomas (Tad) Lincoln

First Lady: 1861-1865

Died: July 16, 1882

Place of Burial: Oak Lawn Cemetery, Springfield, IL

Wardrobe Mis-Functions

Mrs. Lincoln and the World Stage

Mary Todd Lincoln was the same age as two very prominent international celebrities—Queen Victoria of England, and the Empress Eugenie, the wife of Napoleon III. The English monarch was never considered a fashion plate (and after Prince Albert died in late 1861, wore perpetual mourning for the rest of her long life), but the French Empress, a Spanish beauty with a willowy figure, set the fashion world on edge with her dazzling sense of style. It was she who almost single-handedly doubled the yardage needed for a lady's gown when she introduced the voluminous hoop skirts of the 1860s to show off her tiny waistline. Thereafter, at least twenty-five yards of fabric was needed to cover the whalebone or metal hoops that no woman would dare be without.

When Mrs. Lincoln first arrived in Washington as First Lady-to-be in late February, 1861, she was keenly aware of the fashion influence of the Queen and the Empress. As the wife of the President of the United States, she considered herself their peer.

Mary's introduction to Washington society was blindsided by three strikes already against her that she did not realize. Several Southern states had already seceded by that time, with more to follow, as the boiling waters of Civil War were about to overflow within weeks. Those facts she knew; it had been in all the papers for months.

But she did *not* know that the Northerners perceived her to be a Southerner, or at least a Southern sympathizer. Slave-owning, Kentucky-bred, Illinois-wed Mary had several Todd siblings, some of whom signed on with the Confederacy as soon as they could. Her allegiances would be suspect for the rest of Lincoln's administration. It was not true, but it made no difference.

Secondly, the Southerners—and Washington was still a Southern town with Southern social influences—perceived Kentucky-bred, Illinois-wed Mary to be *Western*. This implied that her tastes would be provincial, to say the least. It was also not true.

And finally, it must be remembered that Lincoln was a dark-horse president in 1861, with little experience on the national stage. Few knew very much about him, other than the well-publicized fact that he came from humble origins. Most cosmopolitan Washingtonians assumed he had married a woman of his own station.

That part was *not* true either. Mary had been a Kentucky belle, raised in a prominent and well-to-do Lexington family. She was well-educated and socially adept. She considered herself more than equal to the role she would fill.

Mary's First Shopping Sprees

It is a definite fact of First Ladyhood then and now, that extensive wardrobes are essential, given the number of public appearances entertaining requires. It is also important to note that in 1861, dry cleaning did not exist.

One of the quotes attributed to Lincoln shortly after his election, and while they still lived in Springfield, was that "at least we will get some new clothes out of this." Mary would have to upgrade the level of gowns she had worn in Springfield in quantity, style and cost.

The Lincolns had gone to Chicago a few weeks after the election. He, primarily to meet with political advisors; she to go shopping. Chicago had become a serious rival to Cincinnati, Ohio as the cosmopolitan center of the Midwest. But while Mary made several purchases, she no doubt realized that Chicago's best would not be suitable in sophisticated Washington. Another shopping trip was undertaken to New York City, again, prior to the Lincolns coming to the capital. More purchases were made. The merchants were delighted to have the new First Lady's patronage, and just as delighted to offer her unlimited credit.

Mary Comes to Washington

When Mary arrived in Washington and began receiving the dozens of Congressional wives and society matrons who lined up at the Willard Hotel to meet her, she realized that both her Chicago and New York purchases were still insufficient. Washington society was disdainful, and Mary's resentment and quick temper alienated them from the start. Their obvious coolness had a lasting impact on her, and henceforth her attitude seemed to be to make them eat their words. She was determined to out-dress every one of them, and said garments had to be the very best. To Mary, *best* was synonymous with *most expensive*. According to one biographer, Mary's gowns were as vital to her position as General Winfield Scott's gold braid was to his uniform.

Even before Lincoln's inauguration, Mary spent a good part of her time interviewing potential dressmakers. The day after the inauguration, Mrs. Elizabeth Keckley, a well-known Washington mulatto modiste who had made gowns for Mrs. Jefferson Davis among others, came to the White House for the first time. She would be a fixture there for the next four years.

Mrs. Keckley's job was simple enough: make Mrs. Lincoln soar to the top of the 1861—and thereafter—Best Dressed List. The fabrics had to be the finest; the trim and accessories the most elegant. And even though she professed that the Lincolns were not wealthy and she needed to be mindful of price, nothing but the best would do. Within the next few months, Mary ordered an additional sixteen gowns in addition to the many purchases she had just made in Chicago and New York.

It was inevitable, considering the lukewarm popularity of Lincoln, the Civil War, and of Mary herself, that the extent of her purchases, both in quantity and price tag, would be the subject of gossip. Statements of her extravagance were published in the newspapers. Some articles claimed her gowns cost $1,000 each; some said $2,000. We may never know for sure, except that it was 1860s money, worth at least ten times that amount today.

That there was a war on and soldiers needed shoes and blankets did not seem to matter to Mrs. Lincoln, who only months earlier had been a pleasant looking middle-aged, middle-class housewife from Illinois. She relished being fawned over and flattered for her impeccable fashion sense. New York and Philadelphia merchants were no fools. They soon realized that the quickest way to gain the First Lady's favor was to remark on her excellent taste. They also knew that the more they flattered, the more she purchased, and always top of the line.

The End of the Fashionista

In early 1862, Mary's shopping had become fodder for the gossip mills. Not only did she shop for herself, but she shopped for the White House as well. It had legitimately become rundown and shabby over the past decade, and she was determined that the House of the President be up to snuff. Congress obliged with $20,000, a generous allowance. Still, she went overboard by nearly fifty percent, and even the good-natured and usually indulgent Lincoln lost his temper with her *flub-dubs* as he called them.

Then tragedy struck. In February, eleven-year-old Willie Lincoln died of typhoid, and a grief-prostrated Mary Lincoln wore only mourning attire for two years. It would not be until mid-1864 that she began to include some color in her wardrobe again.

That did not last very long either. A year later, the unthinkable occurred. Mary's husband, Abraham Lincoln, was assassinated.

From that day on, like Queen Victoria, Mrs. Lincoln wore only black. Style and fashion no longer mattered.

Mary's Bad Hat Story

Mary Lincoln definitely knew what she wanted, especially when she became First Lady. She wanted to be the leader of society, the leader of fashion, and the one woman in Washington whose taste and style would be admired and emulated. Nothing was too good for her, so she believed.

The new First Lady had purchased a new gown with purple flowers. It was a very deep and rich shade of purple, and she want the ribbons on her new bonnet to match exactly. Her milliner was understandably anxious to curry the First Lady's favor, but could not obtain that particular shade of purple. The dye-lot for the color had been exhausted. The picky Mrs. L. was not happy, and no alternative suggestion was satisfactory.

It so happened that Mrs. Lincoln shared the milliner with a Mrs. Horatio Nelson Taft, a Washington matron of her acquaintance, and whose two sons, Bud and Holly, had become bosom buddies of the Lincoln boys, Willie and Tad. Mrs. Taft came to one of Mary's receptions wearing a new bonnet with purple ribbons in exactly the shade Mary wanted. The First Lady made a beeline for her and remarked excitedly about the beautiful purple ribbons on her hat. She continued, remarking that *their* milliner claimed no more ribbon of that shade was available. Then she demanded that Mrs. Taft cut the ribbons off *her* hat and give them to Mrs. Lincoln. She obviously believed that her exalted position as the President's wife entitled her to such liberties, but Mrs. Taft was stunned by the effrontery.

It was only after *their* milliner promised to make a brand new hat for Mrs. Taft *free of charge*, that the Washington matron was seduced into handing over the purple ribbons for Her Maryness' pleasure. As one might expect, Mrs. Taft's opinion of Mrs. Lincoln cooled considerably.

But after only a year into her reign as First Lady, Mary's eleven-year-old son Willie died, and a grief-prostrated Mrs. Lincoln put away all her new clothes and hats, including the one with the purple ribbons. Always self-absorbed, Mrs. Lincoln then wrote to Mrs. Taft, instructing her *not* to send her two sons to play with Tad at the White House anymore. She claimed it would be too upsetting for *her*. Nine-year-old Tad never saw the Taft boys again. He no longer would have playmates.

This hat story was told years later by Julia Taft Baynes, Mrs. Taft's daughter, who would pen some of her memoirs of the Lincoln White House in a little book called *Tad Lincoln's Father*. As a teenager during those years, she had often accompanied her younger brothers while they played with the Lincoln boys. She included the hat story, no doubt told to her by her mother.

Curiously enough, however, and despite the colossal nerve of the self-centered Mrs. Lincoln, Julia Taft would actually grow to like her very much.

$\mathcal{S}$eed $\mathcal{P}$earls

$\mathcal{A}$braham Lincoln, child of humble beginnings, was no connoisseur of fashion, let alone ladies' fashion or jewelry. When he first met Miss Mary Todd, he was a gangling lawyer with ill-fitting clothing covering his six-foot-four frame. But Lincoln was no fool. He no doubt realized that if he were to achieve any success as an attorney or public figure he would need polish. Mary Todd was well equipped to do the polishing. As a Kentucky belle from a well-to-do family, she knew what would be needed, and polish she did.

She made a nice middle-class home for them, a place where Lincoln could be proud to bring his associates. She made sure his suits were tailored better, and his hat and coat were brushed daily. She made sure his boots were blacked regularly, and his shirts were freshly laundered and ironed. She taught him to dance a little, make a courtly bow, and balance a delicate teacup on his bony knees. Thus when he was elected President, Abraham Lincoln was socially fit for the parlor, and he undoubtedly knew that he owed a great deal to his society-minded wife of eighteen years.

In February, 1861, as the train brought the Lincolns to Washington for the inauguration, they stopped in New York where the President-elect visited Tiffany & Company, then as now, one of the premier jewelers in the country. As a gift for Mary—one of the few actually recorded as *his* gift—he purchased a stunning set of seed pearl jewelry, to include a necklace and two cuff-style bracelets. The price tag was a whopping $530, an enormous amount in the mid-nineteenth century, especially for someone whose pre-election income was around $6,000 per year, a substantial but hardly opulent sum.

The Pearl Jewelry

The necklace itself was a choker style, defined as a length of fourteen-to-sixteen inches. It consisted of nineteen oval-shaped rosettes, six large and thirteen smaller. One of the six is extra-large, used in the center of the necklace to dangle a somewhat smaller rosette as a pendant. The small rosettes feature a bar of three pearls surrounded by a circle of seed pearls. The larger ovals feature a bar of three pearls surrounded by two seed pearl circles. The extra-large central rosette has three circles of pearls.

The two identical bracelets feature the same rosette style as the necklace, but the central oval rosette is the largest one in the entire set: three large pearls surrounded by four rows of seed pearls. Two smaller (three rows of surrounding pearls) rosettes flank the central piece. The strap and clasp are made of silver plate.

Some historical accounts claim Lincoln also purchased earrings and a brooch, and indeed a similar set, also made by Tiffany's, did include the additional pieces and sold for $1,000. To completely confuse historians, the photograph of Mrs. Lincoln wearing the jewelry shows her wearing the earrings and the brooch. But the paperwork indicates that Lincoln was more thrifty, and opted for the less-expensive set. Perhaps the brooch and earrings were on loan.

Tiffany's Billing Department

The really curious part is that Tiffany records indicate that Lincoln purchased the items on April 28, 1862, more than a year after his inauguration, when it is documented that Mary actually wore them. A Matthew Brady photograph was taken of the new First Lady wearing her inaugural gown, the seed pearl necklace, one of the bracelets, the brooch and earrings. Tiffany may have had *the slows* in its billing department, particularly as it regards presidents. It happens.

It is also possible that when purchases are made and billing does not occur until months or even a year later, the purchaser tends to forget that the purchases are unpaid. Many of the bills for Mrs. Lincoln's personal items, and even for White House furnishings, were not sent until months after the goods had been received.

In addition, the chief occupants of the White House were always recipients of any number of gifts, from the ubiquitous flowers and confections, to great wheels of cheese. The Lincolns, for instance, frequently received baskets of whiskey and other spirits, most of which they sent to the hospitals for medicinal purposes. Lincoln personally received dozens of presentation canes, handy items that were always custom-made to accommodate his height. By the 1860s, railroad passes were commonplace gifts to legislators of all rank. The President's family *never* had to pay carfare. Nor hotel bills. Nor most of their meals when traveling. So perhaps, if a bill is not submitted in due course, it might have been assumed to be a gift. There were no laws against it in the 1860s.

It is also interesting to note that in April, 1862, the date of Tiffany's billing accounts, the Lincolns were in deep mourning for their son Willie who had died a few weeks earlier. The deeply bereaved mother would not have been purchasing or wearing elaborate jewelry.

Alas, there is no documentation of Mrs. L's reaction when she was presented with the expensive jewelry, but one can assume she was *very* pleased. She wore it at both of Lincoln's inaugural balls.

And while the set was a gift from Lincoln, it was definitely *not* a gift from Tiffany's. Lincoln paid the bill personally, once he got it.

The Aftermath of
the Seed Pearl Jewelry

The widow Mary Lincoln made a simple will in 1873. She left everything, to include some property and all her personal possessions, including jewelry, to her son Robert.

The sad circumstances that caused Robert to have his mother tried for insanity (later reversed) understandably created a major rift between them, and they were more or less permanently estranged for the rest of Mary's life.

At the time Mary made her will, she had only seen one grandchild—Robert's daughter Mary, her namesake, nicknamed Mamie. She was only a toddler. Robert's two other children, Abraham II, nicknamed Jack, and Jessie had not yet been born. Mary would never see them in her lifetime.

Despite the estrangement and the fact that she lived nearly another decade, Mary never changed that will. Her property went to Robert. It included the seed pearl necklace and bracelets.

The jewelry is now part of the Library of Congress collection. It was given in 1937 as a gift from Mary's granddaughter, Mary Lincoln Isham, shortly before her death. She was the only grandchild Mary Lincoln ever cuddled.

$\mathcal{M}$ary $\mathcal{L}$incoln's $\mathcal{F}$lannel $\mathcal{P}$ajamas

The Widow Mary

$\mathcal{W}$hen Abraham Lincoln was assassinated in April, 1865, his forty-six-year-old widow was devastated, and despite surviving another seventeen years, she would never completely recover.

Mary Lincoln had no one to turn to for the bottomless amount of emotional support she required. She was completely or partially estranged from her many siblings. No one rushed to comfort her that April. Her oldest son, Robert, was twenty-one, and now man of the family. He needed to put his own life in order before he could even begin to tend to his mother's myriad of problems. Her youngest son, Tad, was only twelve, and somewhat babyish at that. Tad had been born with a cleft palate, a condition that today is routinely repaired in infancy, but impossible to correct in the mid-nineteenth century. Tad had a disabling speech defect. It was coupled with a childhood dyslexia, and the permissive parents had allowed Tad to remain a child as long as he could. The tragic death of the Lincoln's middle child, Willie, three years earlier, had been devastating for the entire family, and particularly hard on Mary. She had only recently begun to emerge from her profound grief when Lincoln was shot.

By the summer of 1865, when the Widow Mary was finally able to resume some semblance of life, she had two major goals. First, to attend to Tad's woefully neglected education; now thirteen, he *still* did not know all his letters. The second goal was to protect her deep secret—thousands of dollars of debts she had incurred as First Lady. She had every intention to repay, or otherwise ameliorate, those obligations but it was a huge strain.

Mrs. Lincoln in Europe

In an effort to escape from financial embarrassment, to find less expensive living arrangements, and to enroll Tad in a good school, Mary went to in Europe in 1868. They moved frequently, but mostly they were based in Germany where education was reputed to be the best on the continent.

With no home of her own, she lived in rented hotel apartments, near Tad's school, wherever it was. With little to occupy her idle hours, an unrelenting depression, and no real friends of her own for comfort or companionship, Mary became hypochondrical, centering on her own health to the extreme.

She had suffered from migraine headaches of varying severity nearly all her life. She had also developed the ubiquitous woman's problems, covering a gamut of symptoms following Tad's birth. At fifty, she was unquestionably menopausal. Now she began to suffer from vague chills and fevers, agues and indefinable malaise. She consulted several doctors during the three years she lived in Europe. Most of them recognized the underlying emotional cause of these ailments.

Psychiatry had not yet become a medical discipline of its own. Sigmund Freud was three years younger than Tad. Nevertheless, there was a growing interest on both sides of the ocean in the treatment of diseases of the mind, and no doubt Mary Lincoln's doctors believed a good deal of her problems were emotionally exacerbated. They were at a loss for what to do. She was a difficult patient, not only to diagnose, but to treat.

In desperation, some of them suggested a warmer climate. She went south. After a while, the doctors there sent her back to cooler climates. She returned north. Nothing was going to help.

The Pajamas

Finally, during one of her chills-and-fever episodes, one of her German physicians suggested that she sleep in flannel pajamas.

It is not as strange as it might seem. Hotel rooms in the 1870s were damp and drafty, especially the older ones that may have been decades old by the time Mary lived there. If there was such a thing as central heating, it was primitive and flawed. Most heating was done via fireplace and stove. Whatever the reason for Mary's ailments, the cold and damp rooms were certainly not helping. Warm pajamas, rather than cotton nightgowns, might provide additional warmth, a universal antidote to chill.

Pajamas had become popular in Europe. They had originated in India and had been brought back by the British colonists in the Asian sub-continent. The loose-fitting comfortable garments were worn by both men and women.

So Mary sent Tad out to the store to buy her some flannel pajamas. It is impossible to know what they actually looked like. Women's nightclothes were in the unmentionables department. One can assume, however, that they were *not* red, and were *not* decorated with bunnies, ducks or penguins. However, one can easily imagine an unbearably embarrassed sixteen-year-old boy with a speech defect asking a merchant for flannel pajamas for his mother. But he bought them.

They had been doctor prescribed, and Mary would wear them intermittently for the rest of her life.

$\mathcal{J}$ULIA $\mathcal{B}$OGGS $\mathcal{D}$ENT $\mathcal{G}$RANT

Born: January 26, 1826

Place of Birth: St. Louis, MO

Parents: Frederick Dent; Ellen Wrenshall Dent

Marriage: August 22, 1848

Children: Frederick Dent Grant; Ulysses Simpson (Buck) Grant;

Ellen (Nellie) Wrenshall Grant Sartoris Jones; Jesse Root Grant

First Lady:1869-1877

Died: December 14, 1902

Place of Burial: Grant's Tomb, New York, NY

Julia's Bad Hat Story

This is Julia's own story, the one *she* tells herself in the memoirs she wrote more than a century ago, and which had remained tucked away in a granddaughter's attic for some seventy-five years. Perhaps a key to Julia's social popularity was her ability to laugh at herself—or, if not to actually laugh, to present herself in an embarrassing light with insouciance.

Julia Dent Grant was a genuinely nice lady. Most people liked her, possibly *because* she was plain in looks, somewhat dowdy in style, and neither exceptionally brilliant nor intellectual, nor witty. In other words, she was no threat to the grand dames of society. They flocked to her and embraced her sincere and natural pleasantness.

For all her finishing school advantages, Julia Dent was generally sheltered and in some ways naïve. As a child, she completely relied on her father to make all decisions. Once she married, she relied on her husband to do likewise, including all things political. *Sort of.* During the Civil War, of course, General Ulysses S. Grant was occupied with far more responsibilities than worrying about his wife's choices of fashionable headgear.

Early in the war, when Grant was a general, but not *the* General, Julia was staying near Cincinnati, Ohio and was in need of a new fall bonnet. A cousin took her shopping, and she spied a charming hat in nut brown, decorated with red and white cut velvet flowerets. It was probably becoming, matched her winter coat, and the price was within her means, the usual criteria for bonnet purchase. She bought it and proudly wore it in public. She was surprised however, by the snickers and whispers, nods and smiles as she passed acquaintances on the street.

Julia had no idea that in 1862, nut-brown with red and white cockades was the symbol of the Confederacy, and thus a way for the fair sex to tacitly register its political allegiance, even in Union territory. She quickly learned that bit of information. Even though Julia was definitely a Southerner, her Missouri-born-and-bred Western claims notwithstanding, and a slave owner to boot, it had never occurred to the non-political woman that her hat was making a statement, and the wrong one at that. Naturally, a high-ranking Union general could not have his wife espousing the enemy's cause, tacitly, overtly or even accidentally.

Julia was mortified. She never wore the hat again. She immediately purchased another bonnet in a safe style and color arrangement. She also took her shopping companion to task for neglecting to alert her about the previous symbolic *faux pas*. "But I thought you knew," her cousin protested. Friends always say that.

Julia truly did *not* know those implications. Her political knowledge was sincerely naïve. She had made a couple of political slips before, and would make more. But she would learn a valuable lesson; she kept her mouth shut about public matters from then on, and shopped more cautiously. She learned that when you are married to a public figure, you become an extension of his image. You are watched closely. Everything you do and say is open for public criticism, and the public will always criticize. It becomes the fishbowl life that every First Lady has railed against at some point, and it is not likely to change.

What is particularly refreshing however, is that Julia Grant chose to air her tidbit of slightly soiled laundry *herself* more than three decades after it happened, and after she had become somewhat iconic in her own right. She could have forgotten about it. She could have written nothing about it and no one would have ever been the wiser. But she didn't. She included her *oops* moment without self-consciousness, and laughed at herself. Perhaps that is why she was so popular, both in and out of the White House.

The Suitcase

*J*ulie Dent Grant was no looker by any stretch of the imagination. Her plainness was compounded by an eye condition from birth called *strabismus* in the medical profession. Most people know it as being *cross-eyed*. Today, this slight defect is usually corrected in early childhood, but in 1826, when Julia was born, there was no cure. She was understandably sensitive about it, but she never permitted her wandering eye to stand in her way of social opportunities. Fortunately for her, she had a warm and pleasant personality, and would make friends easily, both male and female.

When she graduated from her St. Louis finishing school at seventeen, she met Second Lt. Ulysses S. Grant, a recent graduate of West Point who had been a roommate and close friend of her brother Fred. It was love at first sight for both of them.

The Grant Marriage

Grant was redeployed a few months after he and Julia had met. They had become secretly engaged by that time, but four years would pass before they finally married. The couple enjoyed nearly forty very happy years together, sharing four children and some monumental ups and downs.

Following three years of routine military barracks life, Grant was once again redeployed out West. Julia, now carrying their second child, returned to St. Louis, and the care of her family. Traveling to California across the Isthmus of Panama in the early 1850s was no place for a pregnant woman and two-year-old toddler.

Grant fared poorly out West. He was ill-suited to the quartermaster duties assigned to him and was abysmally homesick. In his depression, he began to drink. He was ushered out of the military, being told to either resign or be sacked. He resigned and returned to St. Louis.

Then came nearly ten years of wandering in his desert of limbo. Grant could not find suitable employment, and whatever occupation he did get was short-lived. Bad luck followed them. Through it all, Julia was his stalwart companion. She never complained or displayed disappointment, not even with a look. She believed in the greatness of her husband throughout.

The Civil War years, and Grant's rise to immortality, is well known. During those four years of war Julia was a nomad, with four small children in tow. Wherever Grant was stationed for any length of time, Julia and the gang would be summoned, and there she would make her temporary home.

By the end of the Civil War, and particularly after the death of Lincoln, Grant was *the* man of the hour, and arguably the most important and popular person in the country. All the rich and famous flocked to Grant and his "plain little wife," as she called herself. His election as president in 1868 was practically taken for granted, no pun intended.

Julia's Suitcase Story Begins

Mrs. General Grant had also become an important personage in her own right, and plain or not, she was popular. It had been more than a half-century since social life in Washington dazzled under Mrs. Madison. Few could remember those days. Subsequent First Ladies did not, could not, or would not measure up. The four years of Civil War and the national despondency over its huge casualties had all but reduced formal entertaining to small dinner gatherings and the obligatory mundane receptions. The four years of Andrew Johnson's troubled and antagonistic presidency were further depressed by his wife Eliza, a tubercular invalid. Johnson's two daughters did a creditable job, but the mood was sour.

Enter the Grants. They were popular. They were more than popular. They were idolized and practically beloved. Even in the devastated South, Grant was regarded better than somewhat for his magnanimity and judicious treatment. Congress was delighted. The Republican Party was not only in power, they were in mega-power. And fashionable entertainment at a Gilded Age White House in the spotlight was on the A-list of go-tos.

It was natural then, that Mrs. Grant should become acquainted with a wide range of citizens, including some well-known physicians. She came to learn that her eye problem could now be corrected, and she was interested. Extremely interested. As First Lady, her photograph was in demand, and Julia had spent a lifetime shunning the camera. The rare photographs of her were always taken in profile.

Mid-nineteenth century photography was still a complexity of art and science. The subject was required to sit very still while the photographer and camera did their magic. Julia could sit still very nicely, but she could not control her eye muscle from wandering at will.

Spurred by the revelation that her eye condition could be repaired, she sought further consultation. She was again reassured that the weak muscle could not only be corrected, but it was no longer considered a difficult or dangerous operation. The doctors promised complete success. After serious thought, Julia decided to have the operation and arranged to go to Philadelphia, which at the time had the finest hospitals and doctors in the country. She would spend a week under the care of the finest eye surgeons in America.

It was *her* decision. *She* signed the papers. She made her preparations and she packed her suitcase. Likely she included appropriate nightgowns and wrappers, the nineteenth century equivalent to bathrobes. Likely she packed slippers and brushes and combs and soaps and powders and the usual products for intimate care. Likely she packed an assortment of day-dresses suitable for a medical recovery. She would be ambulatory, but would remain secluded for a week.

Julia was undoubtedly apprehensive about eye surgery, but she bit the bullet. Her husband however, was uneasy about all of this. Grant seldom interfered with Julia's personal decisions, but this one was disturbing him. Shortly before she was ready to depart for the train station, he sent her a note.

> *Dear Julia,*
>
> *I don't want to have your eyes fooled with. They are all right as they are. They look just as they did the very first time I ever saw them—the same eyes I looked into when I fell in love with you— the same eyes that looked up into mine and told me that my love was returned . . .*

Julia cancelled the appointment.
She unpacked her suitcase.
She never had her eye muscle repaired.
She never complained about it again.

LUCY WARE WEBB HAYES

Born: August 28, 1831

Place of Birth: Chillicothe, Ohio

Parents: Dr. James Webb; Maria Cook Webb

Marriage: December 30, 1852

Children: Birchard Austin Hayes, James Webb Cook Hayes,

Rutherford Platt Hayes, Fanny Hayes Smith, Scott Russell Hayes

(3 d. infancy)

Died: June 25, 1889

Place of Burial: Spiegel Grove, Fremont, OH

The *Old-Fashionista*

*M*rs. Rutherford B. Hayes, the former Lucy Ware Webb, is one of those paradoxes of history: The realities and the persona created about her were very different.

Lucy Webb was Ohio-born and raised by a single mother. Her father died when she was a baby. Rutherford Birchard Hayes, Lucy's husband, was a posthumous child, also raised by a single mother, thus creating an additional bond between them, as well as providing strong female influences in both their lives. In Lucy's case, the strong mother was an ardent feminist in the earliest days of feminism. Mrs. Webb was a supporter of Mary Lyon, who espoused higher education for women back in the 1830s and '40s, when the subject was considered bordering the lunatic fringe. But such was her influence that Lucy went to Wesleyan Female College in Cincinnati, and is considered the first First Lady to have received the benefit of higher learning.

She studied the tough subjects: Latin, Greek, algebra and geometry, history and philosophy, science and geography, as well as the more *feminine* subjects like poetry and literature, perhaps a little French, and of course, domestic skills. If she ever utilized that education, it was merely to become a suitable consort for a prominent man, which she did. She married at twenty, and raised five children to maturity.

By her own admission, Lucy considered herself an old fashioned girl. Whatever inclinations her mother may have had regarding feminism, Lucy was not so ardently inclined. She had no ambitions other than being a wife and mother. She favored the high-necked, long-sleeved gowns of her youth rather than the low-cut, bosom-displaying fashions of the Civil War era. Bustles, of course, came later. They were also in the back, and were concealing—not revealing. Those modest styles did not compromise Lucy's devout Methodist faith.

She also favored the same hair style throughout her life— parted in the center, and tied in a low bun at the back of her neck. It was a style far more becoming to Lucy's oval face than it was to Mary Lincoln or Julia Grant, who both wore similar hairdos.

Lucy and the New Woman Image

By 1877, when Rutherford B. Hayes became president, women had begun to assume more visible roles. Lucy undoubtedly had a better education than most, but the truth was that a large proportion of American women had a better education than their mothers and grandmothers. Most were literate by then. Such was their growing influence, that magazines devoted to fashions and homemaking and parenthood had become hugely popular after the Civil War. Women subscribed by the thousands. In the next decade, subscriptions would number in the millions.

Traditional pre-Civil War positions of governess, schoolteacher, seamstress and milliner were now joined by clerks, office assistants, sales personnel, formally trained schoolteachers and nurses, and even journalists—for those massive numbers of Civil War widows and orphaned daughters who needed to earn a living. The invention of the telephone and the typewriter alone drew thousands and thousands of women into the workforce. Then there were small armies of new immigrant women factory workers laboring in pitiful conditions, not to mention huge numbers of domestic servants.

Perhaps because of her higher learning, or perhaps because she was definitely better looking than pouty-faced Mary Lincoln or plain-as-a-post Julia Grant (the tubercular Eliza Johnson didn't count since few people ever saw her), Lucy Hayes, now in her mid-forties, was touted in the newspapers as "the new woman."

So there really *was* such a thing as a *new woman*. But was Lucy Hayes really its personification?

The Hijacking of Lucy's Persona

It was Mary Clemmer Ames, a female journalist who had been around the Washington scene since Lincoln's time, who literally hijacked the new First Lady Hayes' persona. Article after article was published touting her as the ideal woman, mainly to sell newspapers, and it was all done *without* Lucy's permission, expressed or tacit. In those days, permission wasn't required. And for the record, Lucy never solicited the praise nor granted a public interview.

The 1870s was also the emerging heyday of the Women's Christian Temperance Union (WCTU), brandishing axes of war against the demon rum. They too hijacked the First Lady as the guiding icon of *their* cause, again without her permission. Lucy was unquestionably a temperance supporter, and is credited with "banning spirits in the White House." Maybe. Maybe not. Some historians believe it was President Hayes himself who issued the dictum as good moral politics, and let Lucy take the credit—or heat—depending on one's point of view.

Lucy disdained both connections, if not overtly, than by her complete disinclination to say *yea* or *nay*. She also refused to participate in any activity other than the domestic duties she sincerely enjoyed, and were supported by her husband. To her perpetual discredit, she declined an invitation from an old classmate to be the commencement speaker at a small women's college. It has been suggested that the generally shy Lucy had a fear of public speaking, since she subsequently declined other offers of organization leadership, even after her term in the White House. Perhaps. It makes sense. Fear of speaking in public is common, particularly among the bashful.

She was also *never* a member of the WCTU, no matter how much they pestered her to join or emblazoned her in their publications. She said she believed in *temperance,* not abstinence, and that if someone wanted an occasional brandy or a glass of champagne, it was none of her concern.

The story goes that she once voiced her annoyance to her husband about the WCTU and the way they seemed to commandeer her public image. She didn't like it. Hayes was an able attorney, but he was also a political animal. He advised his wife that so long as the temperance ladies told no untruths or offended her in any way (pestering not included), she should let the matter lie. So she did.

The $\mathcal{B}$urgundy $\mathcal{G}$own

$\mathcal{T}$he reward for accepting all this *new woman* and *temperance queen* bleating was an heroic-length portrait of First Lady Lucy Hayes by Daniel Huntington, a well known and highly regarded portrait artist of that period.

For all her disdain of public persona as First Lady, Lucy had her own quiet but passionate interests. She liked art and she liked history. She began to collect portraits of previous presidents, and occasionally had professional copies made of famous ones to hang in the White House. The huge portrait of Martha Washington that hangs across the fireplace from the equally huge Gilbert Stuart (maybe) portrait of George was commissioned during the Hayes administration. Prior to Lucy Hayes, if any portraits of First Ladies were commissioned, they were private, and remained in private hands.

Lucy Hayes' portrait was the first formal First Lady likeness to be created especially for the White House. The story goes that the Women's Christian Temperance Union wished to honor their vaunted heroine, so they specifically asked her to choose a gift she would appreciate and find suitable. *She* was the one who suggested a portrait for the White House, and it was duly commissioned and paid for by the WCTU, which she still declined to join, even after her term in the White House had ended.

The Insightful Artist

Artist Daniel Huntington (1816-1906) was delighted to accept this important commission. He was already renowned for his portraits throughout the country, not only by the public and his long list of satisfied patrons, but by his own peers as well. He also knew that this portrait would be well publicized, and permanently and prominently hung in the White House. He did not disappoint.

He produced exactly what was desired: an elegant depiction of the old-fashioned girl as the *new woman*. It is truly heroic in proportion—over seven feet high. Lucy was around five foot three. She was fifty when the portrait was painted, and had had eight pregnancies. Huntington was not only skillful, but intuitive and insightful, which perhaps contributed to his success as an artist. He managed to subtract a few years and a few pounds, which no doubt pleased Lucy. Her hair style is as it had always been—plain and, on her, attractive. Her gorgeous burgundy velvet gown is high-necked with simple lines and decorous white lace trim. It is also long-sleeved, giving away nothing of the woman behind the gown. Except for the face.

Huntington was able to capture Lucy's inherent warmth and intelligence as well as the modest charm with which she conveniently ducked commenting on current issues. Notwithstanding, the portrait depicts an imposing figure of integrity and decorum. Lucy was a public figure and she knew it. Despite the efforts made to exalt her image, she had every intention of demonstrating whatever moral influence she had in the only way she knew how and the only acceptable way—by influence of a good example. The artist got that part exactly right.

The WCTU happily paid for the portrait, and presented it to incoming President James Garfield shortly after his inauguration, and it was duly hung in the White House. It has been copied many times. It also created a tradition. After the brief Garfield term, and that of the widowed President Chester

Alan Arthur, whose formal presidential portrait was also painted by Huntington, all First Ladies have been painted for posterity, courtesy of the American people. The gallery of First Ladies that began with Lucy Hayes' portrait wearing her exquisite burgundy gown has become a graceful and popular addition to the White House.

FRANCES FOLSOM CLEVELAND

Born: July 21, 1864

Place of Birth: Buffalo, NY

Parents: Oscar Folsom; Emma Cornelia Harmon Folsom

Marriage: June 2, 1886 - Grover Cleveland (1)

Children: Ruth Cleveland (d. age 12); Esther Cleveland
Bosanquet; Marion Cleveland Dell Amen; Richard Folsom
Cleveland; Francis Grover Cleveland

February 10, 1913 - Thomas Jex Preston, Jr. (2)

First Lady: 1886-1889; 1893-1897

Died: October 29, 1947

Place of Burial: Princeton Cemetery, Princeton, NJ

The *Wedding Gowns* *Story*

*I*t was the best kept secret in Washington. Forty-nine-year-old grumpy-looking sitting President Grover Cleveland with a matching disposition was about to be married.

Grover Cleveland could never be considered anyone's *beau ideal*. At nearly three hundred pounds for his five-foot-nine frame, he was the heaviest president until 1885. Only the six-foot-two President William Howard Taft would surpass that size by about fifty pounds. If that weren't enough for a non-Adonis, Cleveland's jowly and mustachioed features seemed to be perpetually set in grouch.

Perhaps he had reason. If there was anything Cleveland disliked, and anything that could make the scowl glower, it was an invasion of his privacy, especially after the ruckus about how he had fathered an illegitimate child a decade earlier. And now, what could be more private than his own wedding? Fewer than fifty invitations were issued, and he wrote them all personally. By hand. The press, which had become extremely intrusive by 1885, was expressly forbidden to attend the small wedding ceremony.

The unlikely bride was the pretty twenty-one-year-old Frances Folsom with a good figure, a peaches-and-cream complexion and dimples. She had recently graduated from Wells College in upstate New York and had just returned from a European trip, where she purchased her bridal trousseau.

Making the story a little more complicated than merely eyebrow-raising cradle-robbing, was the fact that Cleveland had been Frances' legal guardian for more than a decade. Her father, Oscar Folsom, had been his close friend and law partner. When Frances was born, "Uncle Cleve" gave the Folsoms the baby buggy. Folsom died in a carriage accident when Frances was nine, so it was only natural for Cleveland-the-estate-executor to assume guardianship, and see that Frances and her mother had all the comforts of middle-class life in Buffalo.

By the time Frances was a student at Wells College, Cleveland was governor of New York. If letters and bouquets arrived at school for Miss Folsom, it was perfectly natural. It was no secret that the Governor was her guardian. And if Cleveland invited Frances to be his *escort* at a dinner at the Governor's Mansion in Albany, it was only matter of course. She was considered family.

No wonder the President guarded his news of impending nuptials. The quasi-familial relationship could be the stuff of scandal.

The engagement had been a total surprise to Washington society, whose matrons had been intent on introducing the gruff, overweight President to every eligible and equally unattractive widow and old maid in town. But no sooner did Miss Folsom and her mother arrive back in the United States, than the wedding was not only announced but performed a week later. Since the event was to be held in the White House, completely under his personal control, President Cleveland had seen to all the plans himself: the ceremony, the invitation list, the minister and even the wedding vows. His unmarried sister Rose Elizabeth, who had been his hostess for a year of First Lady duties, arranged the menu, the floral decorations and summoned the Marine Band. All the bride had to do was show up for the ceremony—with her wedding gown.

The Gown(s)

The one small concession that President Cleveland made for public consumption about the wedding was a detailed written description of Miss Folsom's wedding gown. After all, nearly every woman in the country, and absolutely every dressmaker in the country, waited with bated breath to learn what the young and pretty new First Lady would wear on her historic wedding day.

Plum assignments went to artists at both *Harper's Weekly* and *Leslie's*, the two major magazines of the day: create the wedding scene complete with an imaginative rendering of Miss Folsom's wedding gown, taken from the public description. The *Washington Post* reported the day after the wedding that

> *The bride wore an enchanting white dress of ivory satin, simply garnished on the high corsage with India muslin crossed in Grecian folds and carried in exquisite falls of simplicity over the petticoat. The orange blossom garniture, commencing upon the veil in a superb coronet, is continued throughout the costume with artistic skill. She carried no flowers and wore no jewelry except an engagement ring, containing a sapphire and two diamonds.*

Yet another description offered this:

> *Frances Folsom was a lovely bride in ivory satin and a long veil; her train was four yards long. Attached to the left side of her gown was a scarf of soft white India silk, looped high and forming an overskirt bordered on the edge with orange blossoms; full folds of mousseline, edged with orange blossoms, were draped across the bodice. Her bridal veil, of white silk tulle, five yards in length, was fastened to Frances' hair with orange blossoms and trailed to the end of her magnificent train. She wore long gloves to meet the short sleeves of the elegant gown.*

Since neither the journalists nor the artists saw the gown, no wonder nobody could really understand what it really looked like.

But one of the important descriptions given to the press was that the bride's gown had an exceptionally long train. Great liberty of expression could be taken from the description-with-long-train. Thus it was no surprise when the very next issues of both *Harper's* and *Frank Leslie's Monthly* carried artistic representations of the wedding scene, but with completely dissimilar gowns. But *both* depictions featured exceptionally long trains.

The Gown Story Continues

Most modern brides, if they choose to wear traditional gowns, either wear a family heirloom, or spend serious money on a one-time dress. Grandma's gown might be altered to fit before its re-use, of course, and then professionally cleaned and packed away after the wedding for more future posterity. Even a brand new gown is likely to share that long-term fate. Bridesmaid gowns are frequently recycled, but it is rare for a brand new wedding gown to be altered for immediate re-use.

But that is exactly what the new bride, now First Lady Frances Cleveland, did. Shortly after the wedding, she had the gown reworked to wear at public receptions. After all, a First Lady is required to attend so many official functions that an extremely large wardrobe is essential. Thrifty-minded Grover Cleveland would likely frown at the one-shot-only expense. So the wedding gown was dyed rose-pink, and the signature long train was removed. Later, Frances had it altered yet again for her formal portrait. One would never have known it had been her wedding gown. Maybe all the confusion from a written description had an ulterior motive: no one would know the difference.

The Smithsonian Institution, which now owns the gown, has made an effort to restore it to its original state as much as possible, but still without the long train. Thus nobody *really* knows what the wedding gown looked like as Grover and Frances Cleveland were saying "I do."

$\mathcal{B}$ustle $\mathcal{S}$tories

$\mathcal{I}$f there were at least *two* versions of First Lady Frances Cleveland's wedding gown, there are *several* renditions of the famous story of her "repudiation of the bustle."

Very young and pretty First Lady Frances Folsom Cleveland was hot copy for the newspapers and magazine journalists when she married a sitting president in 1886. The press seemed to be insatiable in reporting anything and everything she did, and the American public had a ravenous appetite. Frances was good-natured and did not complain about the publicity, but grouchy President Grover Cleveland detested the invasion of his privacy. His marriage and his bride definitely fell into that category. He even went so far as to buy a house in Georgetown to isolate his bride from the intrusions. He did not mind being a commuter.

Meanwhile in the fashion world of the mid-1880s, bustles had been in style for at least a dozen years, replacing the space-hogging voluminous hoopskirts of the Civil War era. The idea of the bustle was that all the fabric that had been covering the hoops was now cleverly bunched and draped into a clump in the back, which gave the wearer just as peculiar a profile as the hoops—only different. Frances Cleveland was undoubtedly a modest and sensible young woman. She was disinclined to make waves in any aspect of life. That included fashion. If bustles were what women wore, she wore them too. So be it.

The main bustle story claims that there had been no news about the First Lady for a few days, and the newspaper editors were getting antsy and demanded articles. One journalist manufactured a story that "Mrs. Cleveland Abandons the Bustle." Naturally it created a furor among the nation's dressmakers, the popular new women's magazines, and shop owners and their customers. They insisted that Mrs. C. confirm or deny the statement. She received hundreds of inquiring letters. Rather than cause the errant reporter to lose his job if the fabrication was revealed, the First Lady quietly ordered a new gown—without a bustle—which led to a major new fashion look within a couple of years: the tailored skirt of the athletic-looking "Gibson girl," made popular by yet another journalist-artist, Charles Dana Gibson.

Variations on a Theme

Another bustle story massages the aforementioned tale to include a consortium of reporters who colluded in the Big Lie. Still another version has the First Lady actually investigating the origin of the tale and confronting its author to demand a retraction. Yet another version has the fabricator as a *woman* journalist. Like most history, it is likely pieces of true. And pieces of not-so-true.

What appears to be consistent throughout is: a) the story was definitely manufactured; b) Frances Cleveland had no special interest in bustles or non-bustles; c) she did not press charges or demand public retractions or any punitive actions that would harm any reporter's reputation; and finally d) she decided some weeks or months later to order a new gown *sans* bustle.

Some modern historians have made exhaustive attempts to get to the bottom line. Was there collusion? Who was involved? Which magazine or newspaper? Which journalists? Did the First Lady even confront the perpetrators? Was there an offer to retract the fabrication? When did Mrs. C. decide to buy a new gown? How many letters did she receive decrying/applauding the fictitious statement?

This may be, of course, a wonderful challenge and coup for an intrepid scholar, but it can ruin a helluva good story by watering the deliciousness down to such a nitty-gritty mundane level that it becomes a footnote rather than an anecdote, and trivializes the importance of Frances Cleveland.

A Moral to the Story

One thing remains clear. Mrs. Cleveland was as hot a ticket in her time as Jacqueline Kennedy was in hers. She was young. She was popular. She was visible. She was as pretty as her grumpy husband was stodgy. Her smile was infectious and her dimples were disarming. Her good looks and nice figure became a model for whatever fashions she espoused, or was believed to espouse.

Her genuine reticence may have been partially due to her own nature, partially due to her extreme youth, being just twenty-one when she became the youngest of all First Ladies. Her husband wanted his wife to be purely domestic, sheltered and "not given to any notions," as he put it. Frances was an obedient and compliant wife. She wasn't given to any *notions*, such as a career, being outspoken or visible to the public, non-domestic, or, perish forbid, a crusader for some unwomanly cause. Cleveland intensely disliked the woman's suffrage movement and indeed all activities that took a woman's time and interest away from her home and family. His sister Rose Elizabeth was an ardent feminist, and she gave him a headache.

Nevertheless, notions or not, anything Frances Cleveland said, did or wore was fodder for the media gristmill of the 1880s and '90s. The more things change, the more they stay the same.

CAROLINE LAVINIA SCOTT HARRISON

Born: October 1, 1832

Place of Birth: Oxford, OH

Parents: John Witherspoon Scott, Mary Potts Neal Scott

Marriage: October 20, 1853

Children: Russell Benjamin Harrison; Mary Scott Harrison McKee

First Lady: 1889-1892

Died: October 25, 1892

Place of Burial: Crown Hill Cemetery, Indianapolis, IN

Carrie's White Glove

Gloves were an essential part of a wardrobe in earlier times. Both men and women wore them. They came in various styles and colors. Some people purchased them dozens at a time, since they were used so often. Formal ones, usually made of kid, could not be cleaned. There was also no such thing as professional manicures. A stiff nail brush for grime, and perhaps an emery board for shape was all that was possible. Nail polish, like cosmetics, was for the stage or worse, bawdy houses. Hands were to be covered. But the white glove, a cotton glove, was different.

Incredible as it may seem today, some women actually *like* housework. The finest compliment you could have paid our grandmothers was that "she was a good housekeeper."

Just about all our early First Ladies were reasonably competent housewives, trained to manage households from earliest childhood. They stayed within their surroundings, cared for their homes, raised their children, and perhaps most importantly, saw to the family's comfort and well-being. Some had done their own menial tasks. Some had servants from the start. Most had acquired at least a modicum of household help by the time they were ready to become the nation's primo housekeeper.

Caroline Scott Harrison, the wife of twenty-third President Benjamin Harrison, was exceptional. She was a talented homemaker in the Martha Stewart sense. She not only was good at housework, but she enjoyed it thoroughly. She was also very creative. She raised two children. She cooked, baked, gardened, canned, sewed, knitted and designed. She participated in civic activities, was president of her woman's club, soloed in the church choir, and found time to paint in watercolors with better than average artistic skill. When china painting became a popular pastime shortly after the Civil War, Carrie became an expert in that new medium. She installed a small kiln in their Indianapolis house, and gave classes to the local ladies.

Needless to say, nothing around a house escaped Caroline Harrison's critical and expert appraisal.

The FLOTUS as Housekeeper: 1889-1892

It was no surprise that one of the first tasks of the new First Lady Caroline Harrison, upon taking up residence in the White House, was to make a comprehensive white-glove inspection. For the uninformed or merely young, a *white glove* inspection was exactly that—complete household scrutiny made wearing white cotton gloves, which immediately identified what needed dusting or other housekeeping attention.

The fifty-seven-year-old Carrie systematically inspected every nook and cranny in the executive mansion from attic to cellar. On her tour of the attic, she discovered a treasure: remnants of china dinner services from past presidents were collecting dust up in the attic. The china-painter in her was intrigued, and she had several pieces brought downstairs for more careful inspection, and a thorough review to discover exactly *which* president they belonged to. It was the beginning of the famous Presidential china collection that has become so popular today.

But Carrie Harrison was not pleased with her inspection, in general. In 1889, the White House was nearly a hundred years old, and in sore need of repair and a thorough cleaning. There were rats. There was dry rot. There was wood rot. There was termite damage. Some areas of the mansion had not been adequately renovated for generations, the kitchen being one of them. Previous First Ladies had been more than content to casually supervise and let paid staff take care of meal preparation and housekeeping duties. Carrie's predecessor, Frances Cleveland, was in her twenties and too busy raising babies and handling her First Lady responsibilities. She did not know how to cook at all! Not so Mrs. Harrison. She was an excellent cook in her own right. And in 1889, what passed for appliances in the kitchen had not been properly updated, in her view, since the Polk administration more than forty years earlier.

A White House Makeover

Benjamin Harrison came to the White House in 1889 with a large extended family. The President and his missus, their married son and *his* family, and their married daughter and *her* family. Then Mrs. Harrison had invited her elderly father to stay with them. He was nearly ninety and had been living with Carrie's widowed sister and *her* widowed daughter. So if Grandpa was coming to Washington, so were her sister and niece. There would be eleven in all, including the babies, but only five bedrooms and one bath. There was no room for guests.

It was also the pinnacle of the post-Civil War industrial age. By the time the Harrisons were Chief Occupants, electric lights had already been around for a decade. New York City had been electrified for years. There was no reason for the White House to be so badly neglected. The new First Lady was definitely dissatisfied.

If the Harrisons were going to lobby for a new stove and icebox, they may as well requisition electric lights, too. It was time, and Congress was amenable. The First Family went straight to the top. They invited Thomas Edison to assess the situation. The great inventor was happy to oblige and personally came to Washington with some of *his* key engineers for *their* inspection. After two days of intensive poking around, they determined that electrifying the mansion was impossible. Edison concluded that the necessary electrical wiring would create a serious fire hazard and the White House could go up like a tinderbox.

Caroline Wants A Palace

Electricity, fire hazard and *tinderbox* are fearful words. So armed with that information, the domestically inclined Mrs. Harrison began a campaign that, at the time, presented great merit—tear down the old mansion and build a new one. Her thoughts were along the lines of the magnificent Schoenbrunn Palace in Vienna—part residential, part executive offices, and part museum to be open to the public. This way it could be properly electrified, installed with modern conveniences plus sufficient housing accommodations and bathrooms, and be free of rodents, rot and repair.

Congress continued to be amenable. As is their eternal habit, they formed a committee. Mrs. Harrison was included and took an active role. Architectural firms were invited to submit plans and bids. At least three of the most prominent firms in the country responded with their drawings, which are in the Archives to this day. They were elaborate, imposing, and very likely what Mrs. H. had in mind.

Congress reviewed the plans, and in a rare instance of collective good judgment, declined. It was not so much the projected price tag, which was steep. The main objection was the potential destruction of deep and intrinsic and irreplaceable national history. George Washington had personally laid the cornerstone of the White House a century earlier. It had been home to Jefferson and Lincoln. It was where Dolley Madison held her famous soirées and saved the portrait of Washington. Charred remains could still be seen from the War of 1812 when the House was torched. This was history that could never be recreated and must never be lost.

It was a wise decision. Congress voted instead to authorize substantial repairs, including whatever steps were necessary for electrification, and all because First Lady Caroline Harrison made a white glove inspection and gave her nineteenth-century equivalent of *What a dump.*

The P.S. to the Story

Modern technology is always changing and improving. Only a dozen years later, the improvements made by the Harrisons were hopelessly inadequate for the Theodore Roosevelts. Another massive renovation was undertaken, inside and outside, including the building of the West Wing, using all the latest building materials. The steep price tag of the Harrison remodeling paled in comparison to what Congress authorized in the new century. (Besides, they liked TR much better than anybody liked ol' Ben.)

But Roosevelt's renovation lasted less than a half century. The stress and strains from years of presidentially gerrymandered add-ons made the White House not only a fire trap once again, but in imminent danger of collapse. It was completely closed down for more than two years during the Truman Administration in order to make it president-worthy again.

$\mathcal{I}$DA $\mathcal{S}$AXTON $\mathcal{M}$CKINLEY

Born: June 8, 1847

Place of Birth: Canton, OH

Parents: James Asbury Saxton; Catherine Dewalt Saxton

Marriage: January 25, 1871

Children: 2 daughters d. infancy

First Lady: 1897-1901

Died: May 26, 1907

Place of Burial: William McKinley Memorial, Canton, OH

Bedroom Slippers

Poor Ida. Only four years into a happy marriage, Ida lost her mother, two babies and her health in very short order.

Ida Saxton McKinley was the daughter of a well-to-do Canton, Ohio banker. Her childhood was happy and privileged. At twenty-three, she married William McKinley, formerly a brevet-major in the Civil War, who had moved to Canton to begin a successful law practice. Ida's family was delighted when The Major proposed to their daughter. The newlyweds were deeply in love, had a baby daughter a year after their wedding day, and everything was going well for them.

Ida's second pregnancy two years later left her with two major physical ailments: phlebitis (blood clots) in her knee, which caused her pain and lameness; and epileptic seizures which colored her life thereafter. At twenty-seven, she required a cane and was forced to curtail most of what would be considered normal activities.

Phlebitis was well-known in Victorian times, and even now is still considered a serious medical condition. There is a dangerous potential for the clots to break apart and travel to the lungs, sometimes with fatal consequences. Today it can be effectively treated, but in 1875, all that could be prescribed was rest, elevation, a cane, perhaps ice, and possibly something for the discomfort.

Epilepsy had been known since Biblical times, but it was a word that bore a stigma. The word *epilepsy* was never spoken in the presence of either McKinley, although the doctors likely knew exactly what they were looking at. Ida's seizures were couched in phrases like *fainting spells* or *a nervous condition*. And while epilepsy is treatable today with careful medication and monitoring, in the 1870s there was no treatment other than heavy opiates and sedatives.

Ida's medical problems also precluded any thought of more children, limiting the McKinleys' private life as well. Then came the final one-two punches—her little baby, who had triggered the decline of her health, was born sickly and died four months later. Soon afterwards, little Katie, the darling of their hearts, sickened and died before her fourth birthday. It had been a horrendous year.

All of this was too much for Ida to handle, and she fell into an understandably severe depression. This in turn developed into what some psychologists might call a relentless personality disorder, consisting of intense self-absorption and a strangulating focus on her husband, the only dear one left to her. She became fixated on McKinley to the point that she could become hysterical with worry if he were detained, even for a short while. This in turn could induce a seizure. Her world became extremely small. Her interests revolved solely around herself, her husband and their life together.

Caring for Ida

Nearly a century and a half after Ida McKinley's health spiraled downwards, one can state with fair certainty that her physical *and* mental health would be greatly helped by modern medical and psychological treatment. She would likely require specialized medication and careful watching even today, but her life surely would be less limited.

In part because he believed a change of scenery would be helpful for both of them, McKinley ran for and was elected to

Congress. He sold their house in Canton with its sorrowful memories, and took rooms at the Ebbitt House Hotel in Washington, since Ida could not assume any household responsibilities. In addition, and at great financial cost, he engaged a full-time nursemaid, since his wife could not be left alone for long periods.

But what Ida required most of all in 1875 was a well-regulated regime. No stress. No demands. And no surprises. This was a major part of whatever treatments were known and available at that time, and the McKinleys spared no expense in consulting doctors. During the next quarter-century, they consulted dozens of them, even traveling to New York and Philadelphia, hoping in vain for a cure to Ida's afflictions.

Ida's Slippers

Needless to say, with so many doors closed to her, Mrs. McKinley needed quiet hobbies and activities to fill her days. One of those hobbies was crocheting yarn slippers. It is estimated that she made more than five thousand pairs during the next thirty years. As a part of the rigid routine of her life, the slippers were always made to the same pattern, and usually in the same gray or blue. She made them in various sizes however, and gave them away generously to friends and family, to friends-of-friends, to casual acquaintances and to total strangers. Thousands of pairs were donated to charity.

During the McKinley presidency, the First Couple denied no legitimate charitable request. A pair of slippers, handmade by Mrs. McKinley, was graciously donated to be raffled or auctioned off. It is said that large sums of money were raised.

Interestingly enough, Ida refused to remain secluded, and relentlessly insisted on participating in her husband's life as much as possible. Most of McKinley's political associates cringed at the thought, annoyed by her strangulating personality more than anything. But McKinley was delighted to indulge his wife at every opportunity. This included travel. Despite gargantuan logistical problems via trains, carriages and unfamiliar settings, since he might need to quickly remove her from public humiliation, Ida accompanied McKinley a surprising amount of time. And always with her crocheting bag and plenty of yarn for making slippers.

Ida adored her gentle and very devoted husband to a point of near monomania. He had sacrificed so much of his own happiness to provide for hers. Framed photographs of him surrounded her in every room, wherever she was. In an odd but touching display of her devotion, she selected one of her favorite photographs of him and carefully sewed it to the bottom of her crocheting bag.

This is not a story; it is a good yarn! The bag exists in the McKinley Museum in Ohio, and yes, McKinley's photograph is neatly affixed to the bottom.

White House Trousseau

*I*da McKinley's father, James Saxton, had been a well-to-do banker in Canton, Ohio, a prosperous town in the years following the Civil War. When he passed away in 1887, Ida inherited nearly $100,000, perhaps equivalent to $2 million today. She was now a wealthy woman in her own right. William McKinley never earned that kind of money.

Always petite, despite the three gargantuan meals the McKinleys usually devoured in their hotel-apartments, Mrs. McKinley loved expensive and ornate clothing. The more lace, the more frills, the more ruffles and flourishes the better. Plus diamonds, her jewel of choice. After early tragedies all but destroyed her, and since there was so little in her frail life to bring her pleasure, her doting husband was happy to indulge her tastes. In William McKinley's mind and heart, she was still and always the girl of his youth—the prettiest girl in Canton, Ohio. He never denied her anything that was in his power to give, and if she liked fancy clothes, sobeit. And, after all, it was *her* money.

When William McKinley was elected President in 1896, Ida, now nearly fifty, decided to treat herself to a brand new wardrobe. Despite her fragile health, she had made it abundantly clear that she intended to fully serve as First Lady, in essence as well as in name. There would be no young nieces to substitute in the social arena, and Ida's demands could never be thwarted without incurring dire consequences to her health. McKinley beamed his approval, much to the apprehension of both his political and personal friends who believed Ida to be a distraction at best, and more likely, a detriment.

So Ida bought day gowns, evening gowns, afternoon gowns, and all the fixin's. Her new trousseau was said to cost more than $10,000. It included eight formal gowns and a headdress made of egret plumes, and would likely rival the adjusted price tag for Mrs. Kennedy's outfits seven decades later, but with little of the latter's classic style.

Ida's taste in gowns was not trend-setting, *a la* her predecessor, the young Frances Cleveland. By the time Mrs. McKinley was in the White House, the *new look* had begun to accentuate the healthy, athletic-looking woman of the emerging twentieth century. Slimming A-line skirts with few petticoats and man-tailored shirtwaist blouses and jackets were popularized by the magazine illustrations of Charles Dana Gibson. They suited Gibson Girls who played golf and tennis and rode bicycles. Frail Mrs. McKinley was far from the picture of robust health, and favored the older fashions of her youth. They were all made of with fine fabrics, and copiously trimmed with so much ribbon and lace that they practically overpowered this wisp of a delicate flower. Ida appeared enveloped by her clothes. One White House visitor commented that she looked too delicate to even lift the rings on her fingers. But she was happy.

The McKinley campaign of 1896 ushered in what many historians believe to be the beginning of the modern age of political publicity. Thanks to the deep pockets of McKinley's closest friend and advisor Marcus A. Hanna, images of the candidate were plastered across America. Photographs of candidate *and* Mrs. McKinley were popular. Ida still maintained traces of her lost beauty. She was still fairly photogenic, on a good day. Newspapers and magazines clamored for information on the new First Lady-to-be whose husband was so devoted to her, a fact not lost on the electorate. It was no secret that she was a semi-invalid and needed a cane. The only secret was the name of her *other* ailment. It was never discussed, merely vaguely couched as fainting spells or a nervous condition.

But McKinley's campaign managers had discovered at least one item about Ida they could happily report to the journalists and their readers: they never failed to mention her new wardrobe and its extravagant price tag. It was the only thing of interest in her limited life that could be shared with the public.

And Ida was delighted by the publicity.

$\mathcal{E}$DITH $\mathcal{K}$ERMIT $\mathcal{C}$AROW $\mathcal{R}$OOSEVELT

Born: August 6, 1861

Place of Birth: Norwich, CT

Parents: Charles Carow; Gertrude Elizabeth Tyler Carow

Marriage: December 2, 1886

Children: Alice Lee Roosevelt Longworth (stepdaughter);
Theodore Roosevelt; Kermit Roosevelt, Ethel Carow Roosevelt
Derby; Archibald Bulloch Roosevelt; Quentin Roosevelt

First Lady: 1901-1909

Died: September 30, 1948

Place of Burial: Sagamore Hill, Oyster Bay, NY

The Cartwheel Hat

By the turn of the twentieth century, styles had changed from the mob-caps of Martha Washington, through the turbans of Dolley Madison and the beribboned bonnets of the Civil War era, fore and aft. Women themselves had changed immeasurably. They were generally healthier, more athletic, eager to participate and find occupation for their time in other-than home and family. The invalidism that protected their mothers and grandmothers was no longer an acceptable alternative. Edith Roosevelt was one of those active women, and while she never joined her husband in his hunting expeditions, she rode horseback with him regularly, rowed and swam in the Long Island Sound, and was game enough to ride camels and elephants in Africa.

To accentuate the new daytime tailored shirtwaists and skirts of the 1900s were cartwheel hats reminiscent of those favored by Marie Antoinette more than a century earlier. They are big, wide-brimmed hats resembling a cartwheel, generously decorated with birds, ribbons, flowers, feathers, and whatever women liked to wear on their heads that year.

Of all the First Ladies married to well-known presidents,

Edith Roosevelt may be the most unique. She shunned the public eye as much as her husband, Theodore Roosevelt, craved it. But Edith loathed the camera as much as Julia Grant, with less cause. There are relatively few photographs of her. Most images, whether visual or in word picture, are the cool woman in a white lawn dress, sewing or reading on the sprawling wraparound porch at Sagamore Hill, their Long Island estate.

During her seven-plus years in the White House, she was popular and busy, and in her own quiet way, left her mark. But perhaps she was much happier to remain hidden beneath her cartwheel hat.

Edith the Cool Lady

Edith Carow had never been an extrovert. Her family had a solid New York pedigree, but her father was an alcoholic, thus the family fortune suffered. Living near the wealthy Roosevelts in New York City would be Edith's great blessing. From earliest childhood, she was included in Roosevelt activities, since her best friend was Theodore's younger sister Corinne. And since all four Roosevelt children were close in age, Edith slipped into the mix effortlessly.

Many people thought Edith and Theodore would marry when they grew up; they had always gotten on famously. They did marry, of course, but not as expected. When Theodore Roosevelt was at Harvard, he fell in love with the beautiful Alice Lee, and married her instead.

Not only did Edith *not* marry Theodore, but her family's financial situation precluded a traditional society debut or college education. Her social standing also precluded any kind of paid employment for her. Her opportunities were limited. Perhaps Edith's metaphorical cartwheel hat served her by hiding her disappointment.

Three years later, Alice Lee Roosevelt died in childbirth, leaving a distraught young husband and a day-old baby daughter, named Alice, for her mother. Two years after that, a now twenty-five-year-old Edith re-met a twenty-eight-year-old widowed Theodore, and the attraction and common interests were rekindled. They married, and would have five more children.

Quintessential Roosevelt Wife

It is fair to ponder what kind of woman would be a perfect mate to a man with such an oversized personality. Edith was unquestionably the brake to TR, the speed-demon. She was also the firm hand on the wheel, guiding the man who needed to be everywhere and do everything. It was Edith who ran the household, managed the family purse (Theodore was always in the spending mode), supervised the children (Theodore was their favorite playmate), and kept a watchful eye and ear on her husband's political exuberance. He needed that in abundance.

Intellectually, Edith was a fine match. Both Roosevelts were voracious readers with book-a-day habits, passed along to their children. While TR's tastes ran toward the sciences, histories and politics, Edith's penchant was for the arts and literature, and novels. Both shared a great love for poetry. It was a fine balance for lively dinner-table conversation.

Perhaps most importantly, Edith gave TR room. He needed a huge amount of independence and personal space for his many and varied interests, most of which took him far afield from home, sometimes for weeks or months at a time. If Edith resented being left to fend with six children, moves between Washington and Sagamore Hill with all the pets and books while her husband was hunting or camping or politicking and having a bully time, it was one more thing she kept under her cartwheel hat.

Perhaps that metaphorical hat also hid her ever-present realization that she had not been Theodore's first choice, and that she was fortunate beyond belief to have married the man she had always loved.

On the other hand, Edith was TR's gentle-but-firm hand of restraint. No slouch in the political arena, she read most of TR's speeches or articles, with a keen eye for spotting those phrases or comments that might provoke too much controversy. If they were in public, her quiet *"Now, Theodore"* would immediately cause him to cease doing whatever seemed to inflame. This was an invaluable service that the ever-impetuous TR needed. His lead-foot accelerator always required a brake, and his directness and occasionally stinging wit required her innate tact.

The Cartwheel Hat with the Plume

Edith Roosevelt was never a fashion-plate image, *a la* her stepdaughter Alice, despite the fashionable cartwheel hats they both wore and both found becoming. It was Alice, the flamboyant *First Teenager* who made the headlines, never Edith, the First Lady. And it was Alice whose styles were reported and copied, and whose color choices were the inspirations for songs. Edith just "looked very nice." If Edith felt envious of the glamor, she never showed it. Her formal White House portrait suits her to perfection—the Woman in White, with a navy jacket, and a plumed, oversized cartwheel hat. White for her privacy, navy for below-the-surface. The artist knew his subject and his craft.

Since Edith hated the camera as much as she hated the limelight, there are very few extant photographs of her before, during or after her years as First Lady. This is all the more remarkable because her husband's photograph was everywhere, and photographic techniques had advanced to a point where candid or unposed pictures could be taken without the subject being aware of it. There are dozens of photographs of the young Roosevelt children while they lived in the White House, but hardly any of Edith, with or without her cartwheel hat.

During Edith's time as First Lady, the White House received a massive overhaul, and as expected, Edith took an active part in both the design and redecoration. Theodore had considerable input in the office construction for obvious reasons, but the White House improvements were all done under Edith's supervision, to include the now-iconic white and gold elegant simplicity of the East Room. She may have taken little credit, and demanded no public acknowledgement for it, but she obviously had taste.

She just wanted to stay aware from the glare, shaded by her cartwheel hat. And it was her choice.

$\mathscr{H}$ELEN (Nellie) $\mathscr{H}$ERRON $\mathscr{T}$AFT

Born: January 2, 1861

Place of Birth: Cincinnati. OH

Parents: John Williamson Herron; Harriet Collins Herron

Marriage: June 19, 1886

Children: Robert Alphonso Taft; Helen Herron Taft Manning,

Charles Phelps Taft

First Lady: 1909-1913

Died: May 22, 1943

Place of Burial: Arlington National Cemetery, Arlington , VA

The Edwardian Gown Story

When William Howard Taft was elected President in 1908, his salary was a huge $75,000 per year. For a quarter-century, he had been a lawyer and jurist whose career was spent in public service. The pay was comfortable but not affluent. For several years, the very wealthy Charles P. Taft insisted on supplementing his younger brother's income to allow him to participate easily in the proper circles. As president, Taft would now be receiving five times more than he had ever earned in past positions.

Mrs. Taft, the former Helen Herron, was always the thrifty family bookkeeper. Called Nellie from birth, she had her eye on reigning in the White House since her teens when she and her parents had spent a week at the Executive Mansion courtesy of family friends Rutherford and Lucy Hayes.

Nellie's marriage to Will Taft was the vehicle to reaching her goal. *She* was the political animal. *She* was the one who made sure the party dues were paid, the good causes subscribed and supported, the people who needed to be entertained were Taft guests, and all advantage taken at the see-and-be-seen occasions. If any skimping was to be done, she tended to skimp on herself.

But she would not skimp during the winter of 1908-09 as First-Lady elect. Will Taft, the three-hundred-plus-pound mountain of a man with the heart of a teddy bear, loved his ambitious wife dearly, and knew he never would have achieved the presidency without her constant eye on the target, and her regular kick in the pants. He himself was ambivalent at best about being president. But it was he who insisted Nellie treat herself to the nifty new wardrobe she deserved. Money was no longer an object. He would proudly tell his military aide, Major Archie Butt, how much he loved "to see his wife well dressed."

The Snappy Looking Mrs. T.

Nellie Taft, at forty-eight, was a fine looking woman. Her features were perhaps a bit sharp, as was her tongue. Nevertheless, she was five-foot-four and had a good figure, perhaps one hundred and thirty-five pounds. Not too thin, not too fat, and barely beginning to gray. If anyone was going to do justice to the glam of Edwardian styles (think early episodes of *Downton Abbey*), it was Mrs. Taft. She was stunning.

Her elegant new gowns reflected the elegance of her new address. High-necked collar adorned with jewels, long sleeves dripping intricate beadwork. The lace, the silks and the fashionable slim lines had been made popular by the slender and graceful Alexandra, Queen Consort of King Edward VII of England. They suited the new First Lady to a tee. It would be one glamorous Nellie who posed for the formal photographs.

Not since Dolley Madison had appeared in a buff gown a hundred years earlier had the time, the place, the fashion and the woman come together so perfectly.

The Sad Looking Mrs. T.

Helen Herron Taft only had a few months to enjoy her gorgeous new gowns and her exciting new life. She had been planning it for decades and knew exactly what she wanted. She replaced horse-and-buggies with automobiles, and organized a *People's Park* in Washington's Tidal Basin with free band concerts, just like the ones she had admired when she lived in the Philippines when Taft was its Governor General. She immediately began to entertain graciously, obviously savoring every moment, just as she had imagined.

Nellie was a complex, tense and driven person all her life. Despite her fine administrative and executive talents, she would still lie awake all night worrying about the decisions she had made during the day. When her People's Park opened, she worried that no one would come. Ten thousand attended the first concert.

But only three months into her husband's administration, Nellie had a stroke that resulted in aphasia, a condition that affects the ability to read, write and speak. To make things even sadder, aphasia does *not* affect the ability to comprehend. Nellie understood everything, and her memory was relatively unimpaired. But she could not communicate or participate in conversation. Even worse, her mouth drooped noticeably, and dining in public was no longer on her agenda.

It took Taft's entire four-year term for her to make a substantive improvement, but as she began to recover she managed to resume a fair amount of First Lady administrative duties. She could make decisions, once they were phrased in the yes-or-no questions she could easily respond to. She could help plan and execute important state dinners. But she was not able to participate.

Taft's military aide, Major Archie Butt, painted a heart-wrenching word-picture of Mrs. Taft, who had planned an elaborate state dinner that she could not attend. There was a small anteroom adjoining the state dining room, and a table-for-one was set with White House china and crystal, silver and flowers. Mrs. Taft, freshly coiffed and wearing one of her elegant gowns, bedecked and bejeweled to the teeth, entered and sat alone, eating the party food she personally had selected. The door to the dining room was left ever-so-slightly ajar, so she could at least hear some of what was being said.

The Fashion Legacy

Perhaps the most lasting contribution among Nellie's several "firsts" (and she managed to have several "firsts" in her three or four months of active participation), was donating her inaugural gown to the Smithsonian Institution, where it remains to this day.

This was the beginning of a tradition that continued through the twentieth century and is not likely to end. Previous First Ladies had articles of their clothing donated before, most provided by their *families*. But never an inaugural gown. Nellie's was the first. And she donated it herself.

The First Ladies collection at the Smithsonian Institution has become one of the most popular and long-running exhibits in the country.

The Silver Chest

Silver is not clothing, but for centuries it has always been in a category similar to jewelry: decorative, elegant items to be treasured and handed down through the generations. It is in this spirit that Nellie's *silver chest,* perhaps considered as table fashion, is included. Besides, it is a nifty story.

A 25th wedding anniversary is traditionally the silver anniversary. Parties have been customary throughout the ages. Thus, when President William Howard Taft and his wife, the former Helen Herron, celebrated their 25th anniversary in 1911, it was acceptable, then as now, for the First Family to host a private party for their special occasion. After all, the White House is their home, if only temporarily.

More than three decades before the Tafts were Chief Occupants, President Rutherford B. Hayes and his wife Lucy had celebrated *their* 25th wedding anniversary in the White House, and had invited family and select friends to join the festivities. Their long-time good friends were the Herrons, who came to Washington with their teenaged daughter, Nellie. She was intoxicated by the charming Mrs. Hayes and by the White House—its glamor, its elegance, its aura of being the seat of power—and perhaps most of all, by the conviction that she, too, might be mistress of the Executive Mansion. That dream would never be extinguished.

When she married William Howard Taft, she had consciously selected a man with the ability and personal talents that could help her achieve *her* goal. She assiduously pursued politics with a one-track mind, channeling her husband's great goal of becoming a Supreme Court justice into her much bigger and better goal, starting with a much better address on Pennsylvania Avenue.

A decade earlier, President McKinley had appointed Taft as Governor General of the Philippines, where he was a huge success. In Manila, Nellie *was* the First Lady, and considered that time as a dress rehearsal for the role she had envisioned for herself in Washington. Throughout her marriage she focused on not only reaching the White House as First Lady, but on all the contributions she would make socially, intellectually and artistically. Her very reason for being had centered on her White House dreams.

She expected to dazzle.

A Party Decision

Part of the reason for the anniversary party in the first place was that it *could* be a "private" affair and one that Mrs. Taft could attend.

Only a few weeks after her husband's inauguration in 1909, Nellie Taft was felled by a stroke. While she was not paralyzed, her disabilities were such that she could not speak properly, nor read and write. Her mouth drooped, preventing her from appearing in public. It had been a depressing year and a half for her, and she had worked tirelessly to regain some of her lost abilities. Taft, who loved his ambitious wife dearly, wanted to give her whatever pleasure he could from her White House experience. Despite the fact that Nellie had aged noticeably, and now preferred comfortable to glamorous, she was enthusiastic with the prospect and participated as actively as she could.

Their Silver Anniversary party had truly begun as an affair for family and close personal friends. Both Taft and his wife had large, close-knit families, each with several siblings-with-spouses and grown nieces and nephews. They *must* all be invited. The Tafts were also social and political animals, and had acquired many friends during those twenty-five years. Of course they *must* be invited.

The Guest List Grows

Somehow this "private" anniversary party began to take on a life of its own—at least regarding the guest list. A president's cabinet is his *official* family. They *must* be invited. Taft's beloved Supreme Court justices *must* be invited. Congressional leadership *must* be invited. Perhaps *all* congressmen and senators as well. The list was growing rapidly.

Both Tafts were Ohioans, with deep personal and political roots. The entire Ohio Republican hierarchy *must* be invited, including the governor, past governors and past leadership. And if the *Ohio* Governor was invited, then all governors *must* be invited, no matter what party.

Military brass, high-ranking administrative executives and the diplomatic corps *must* be included. And one cannot invite a foreign ambassador to such a gathering without inviting his monarch or head of state. The list now included a huge number of people the Tafts had never met, nor were likely to meet, but who *must* be invited anyway. The party plan was out of control.

All told, there were more than eight thousand invitations issued. About seven thousand people actually came to the party.

The Hall of Silver, or the Silver Haul

It is common today for a host to specify "no gifts" or perhaps suggest a donation to a favorite charity. The Tafts made no such requests, however, and since a 25th anniversary is designated a silver one, the gifts began pouring in like a shipment from the Comstock Lode.

They received literally hundreds of silver trays, servers, teapots and tea-sets, urns, platters, serving pieces and candelabra of all sizes and shapes and prices. There were pens, inkwells, desk sets, olive forks, pickle forks, card cases, vanity sets and jewelry for Mrs. T. Many items were monogrammed or specifically engraved presentation pieces. All were of the finest quality, because after all, it was a *personal* gift to the President of the United States. And because it was a *personal* gift, rather than a gift-of-state which belongs to the country, the Tafts got to keep their silver-haul.

According to a tradition of the time, presidential gifts were usually displayed publicly in a room in the White House. Tables were set up, and the silver overwhelmed anyone who was invited to take a look. Guests, visitors and even tourists came to gape. Indeed, the gossip was that invitees would snidely comment on the loot, inquiring amongst themselves just how much did *you* have to cough up?

It had become a very tacky situation, particularly since Mrs. Taft regifted from her stash with abandon. Few objects were ever utilized by them personally. They also sold quite a bit of it during World War I. For bonds, it is said.

Some of it still remains tucked away out of public sight in the Taft Birthplace, now a national historic site, in Cincinnati, Ohio.

$\mathcal{E}$LLEN $\mathcal{L}$OUISE $\mathcal{A}$XSON $\mathcal{W}$ILSON

Born: May 15, 1860

Place of Birth: Savannah, GA

Parents: Rev. Samuel Edward Axson; Margaret Hoyt Axson

Marriage: June 24, 1885

Children: Margaret Wilson; Jessie Wilson Sayres;

Eleanor Wilson McAdoo

First Lady: 1913-1914

Death: August 6, 1914

Place of Burial: Myrtle Hill Cemetery, Rome, GA

$\mathcal{A}$rtist $\mathcal{S}$mock

$\mathcal{E}$llen Wilson was an artist of serious talent, and as is common for an artist, she likely had a smock or two to protect her clothes from paint spatter. But in the metaphorical sense, Ellen's smock covered the artist part and kept it within.

Ellen Axson Wilson lived between wars. Born in Georgia just as the Civil War was about to begin, she died in the White House just as World War I began in Europe. With the South ravaged by war, hers was not a luxurious life, but it sufficed, and Ellen received a better-than-average education. It was her artistic talents, however, that earned her special commendation. While still in high school, some of her freehand drawings were exhibited at a Paris Exhibition, courtesy of one of her teachers traveling abroad. Ellen's efforts won a bronze medal and some local acclaim.

Completely understanding conventional attitudes regarding females, Ellen had little hope of gaining prominence as a professional. Nevertheless, she had some ambitions. Her disposition was not rebellious so she planned to teach art. But even those attainable dreams were cancelled when her mother died. Her father was a Presbyterian minister who was subject to crippling depressions throughout his life. As the eldest of four children widespread in age, it would fall to Ellen to be the family glue.

She was twenty. Her youngest sibling had just been born. She was needed at home, particularly since her father lapsed into one of his chronic melancholies and would never recover.

The Easel Story

There is a story that, like most history stories, has pieces of true. Sometime after her father's death and before she married Woodrow Wilson, Ellen spent a few months in New York City studying at the newly created Art Students League, where they accepted women students and the tuition was free. (That part is definitely true.)

The fuzzy part consists of her being given little attention or instruction from the teachers, since, as a woman, Ellen Axson was expected to marry and raise a family. She would be what was termed a *Sunday painter*. A hobbyist. Not worth much of their time and effort. The story continues that one evening Ellen left an unfinished canvas on her easel, signed only *EA*. The next morning there was a long note pinned to the canvas, praising the work and offering valuable and constructive recommendations. *EA* made an appointment with the teacher, who was surprised the *E* stood for Ellen. Since he could not retract his compliments, and since he could also recognize genuine talent, he began giving her more assistance, and her work steadily improved.

It is a nice story. It would be even nicer if it could be proven definitively. Nevertheless, this is one story that ought to be kept, even if it was semi-embellished. And if there *was* embellishment, it would not have come from Ellen herself. Boasting was against her character and disposition.

A great deal about Ellen Wilson remains hidden, in no small part due to her own modesty and conventional belief in *her place*, which was always a couple of steps behind her husband, whose greatness she believed in with all her heart. It may well be that like Edith Roosevelt, she faded into the shadows of a husband with a powerful intellect and personality. Then too, like another Mrs. Roosevelt who obscured Edith's name and accomplishments from posterity, there would be another Mrs. Wilson as well, doing the same thing to Ellen.

But in the art world, Ellen stood on her own two feet, and stood tall. While she may never have posed serious competition to the more renowned painters of her generation, her artistic talents were always well regarded. She gained the respect and admiration of many American impressionists in the early twentieth century. Ergo, any encouragement she might have been given at the Art Students League would not have been misplaced or patronizing. And perhaps if she had had more time to devote to her art, she might have soared higher. One relative commented on seeing her in her little studio-room, painting away, oblivious to the time as if nothing and no one else even existed. She could focus.

EAW: Artist

Later in her life, Ellen Axson, now Mrs. Governor Woodrow Wilson, entered and won awards in blind competitions where the artists' names are withheld from the judges. By the time she became First Lady, her work was managed by an agent and displayed and sold in well-known galleries, and not merely because she was Mrs. President Wilson. Anyone seeing her watercolor landscapes will immediately recognize their quality on a much higher-than-hobbyist level. Her *real* artist smock was obviously worn frequently.

Ellen's metaphorical smock covering the artist within is another matter. She had voluntarily forsaken any artistic ambitions to become the wife of young Professor Woodrow Wilson, and raise their three daughters, all born within five years, and a string of assorted Woodrow, Wilson and Axson relatives who moved in for extended visits. From the start, the young couple never had an empty house. Being the wife of a complex and complicated man like Woodrow Wilson was a demanding enough career by itself. But Ellen never complained about her alternative life, claiming to have "bartered for something better." She believed wholeheartedly that she had married an exceptional man, and true to her Presbyterian upbringing, a man of destiny. She was contented in the sphere of his undeniable love.

But talent, whether pursued or dormant, does not die, nor does it lie quietly. It seeps out, it bubbles out, and sometimes erupts violently, despite all efforts to contain it. So it was with Ellen Wilson. She painted when she could spare an hour or two. Then, as her daughters grew and became less dependent on her, and as Woodrow Wilson's career developed in ways she could never have imagined, her talents blossomed with the luxury of a few undemanded hours of her own.

Her summer sojourns at artist colonies in New England warmed her soul in a place where she mixed colors with equally gifted peers. She could find that intensely private fulfillment that only she could provide for herself. It could neither be bartered nor bought. Under her artist smock, it was hers alone, and hers to keep.

Ellen's Brown Dress

The story goes that circa 1900, when Woodrow Wilson was the president of Princeton University, his wife was invited to a professors' wives function. One of the ladies attending the party remarked that she had never met Mrs. Wilson, and was looking forward to it. Her companion said that she hadn't arrived, but "you will know her when you see her. She will be wearing a brown dress."

"How could you possibly know that?" asked the first woman.

"She always wears a brown dress," explained the second woman. "It's her best dress, and I think she has only the one."

It is probably a piece of true.

The True Part

Ellen Axson, a Georgia minister's daughter, came from modest means, made even skimpier following the Civil War. Artistic and talented, she had learned to sew as a young girl, owned a sewing machine, albeit a mechanical and cumbersome model, but nevertheless had become an accomplished seamstress. Her creative eye and talented fingers no doubt enabled her to *design-by-ear,* and her petite frame assured that she would always present a fine figure of a woman. Her sewing skills were good enough for her to make her own wedding trousseau.

When Ellen Axson married Woodrow Wilson in 1885, he was just beginning his academic career. Even though he got off to a flying start in scholarly circles and fast-tracked thereafter, professors do not earn fortunes, then or now. By the time the Wilsons had been married for five years, they had three daughters. Ellen's young brother, about nine years old at the time of the Wilson marriage, came to live with them from the start. Another teen-aged brother visited periodically. An assortment of other relatives on both sides of the family would stay for long-term visits. Money was obviously always tight.

For two decades Woodrow Wilson supplemented his modest income by writing a book nearly every a year, always well-received, but best sellers only in limited academia. He regularly accepted extra engagements for seminars and lectures at various universities. In his chosen field of governmental studies (political science, in today's vernacular) he was both prominent and well-liked but he worked hard and continuously.

Somewhat paradoxically—since artistic talents and practicality do not usually coincide naturally—Ellen was the bookkeeper in the family. Woodrow disliked number-work, and was relieved to have his efficient and capable wife look after those mundane details. Her priority was Woodrow's health. Period. It was always fragile. His delicate constitution required periodic rest and recuperation from his exhausting pace. Naturally, those expenses immediately moved to the top of the budget. Then came his books and professional expenses. Then came the children's needs, and the needs of everyone else in the family, including their health and education, which presented their own economic problems.

Finally, if there was anything left over, Ellen might actually spend something on herself. That was seldom. She needed little. She continued to make her own clothes plus all her daughters' clothing. Her talented hands were never idle. And if and when she could not afford a new gown, she would rework an old one with new trim to make it *look* new, just like most middle-class women in the country had been doing for years. She once remarked proudly that she spent only $3 to make a brand new evening gown for herself. Thus, perhaps, the seeds for the brown dress story.

Sewing for Ellen Wilson was relaxing, particular the hand-done trim part. In the days before radio and television, her husband or someone else would read aloud while she sewed or knitted.

It would not be until 1912, when Woodrow Wilson was elected President of the United States, that Ellen and her now-grown daughters finally purchased store-bought clothing, or at least gowns made by professional dressmakers. As First Family females, the Wilson women required large and impressive wardrobes. Their presence would be in demand, and then as now, they would be inspected from head to toe. Meanwhile, Wilson's finances had improved greatly. The presidential salary of $75,000 was considered munificent.

It is noted, however, that the gown Ellen wore to her husband's inauguration was also brown. It is rather doubtful that it was the same brown dress of her Princeton days so many years earlier. Maybe she just liked brown.

FLOTUS Ellen Wilson

More importantly, the new First Lady no longer had time to devote to dressmaking. She had to entertain at an exhausting pace, sometimes three or four hundred people in a single day. She became active in a slum-clearance project, making dozens of visits to affected neighborhoods, scores of telephone calls and hosting special teas and luncheons to lobby for her pet cause. Meanwhile, she found some time to work with the White House gardeners to design the Rose Garden, in what she considered a perfect spot she discovered on her first day as First Lady.

Ellen Wilson had places to go, people to see, a White House to oversee, a family that still needed her—including White House wedding plans for two daughters—and a husband who relied on her heavily. He never made a speech nor wrote an important letter or paper without her input. What precious little personal time she had would now be spent at her easel. Her artwork was gaining substantive prominence. Her landscape watercolors were being shown in major galleries and museums. Others could make her gowns. No one else could paint her pictures.

But unbeknownst to anyone, including herself, Ellen Wilson's health was failing from Bright's Disease, a serious kidney ailment. With no antibiotics, it was an absolute killer in the early part of the twentieth century. Modern historians and physicians believe she may have developed the disease after the birth of her last daughter some twenty-five years earlier. As her fifty-four-year-old body began to slow down with the demands of her new office, she likely blamed her weariness on her age and hectic schedule.

It took an accidental fall in her room (not overly serious on its own) to induce her body to say *enough*. When she did not respond adequately to the customary treatment, her doctor looked further. It did not take long to discover the root cause of her decline. She ebbed and flowed for a few months, but mostly ebbed.

First Lady Ellen Wilson died in the White House just as the first guns of the Great War were about to boom.

*E*DITH *B*OLLING *G*ALT *W*ILSON

Born: October 15, 1872

Place of Birth: Wytheville, VA

Parents: Judge William Holcombe Bolling; Sallie White Bolling

Marriage: (1) Norman Galt (1896) - No children

(2) Woodrow Wilson (December 18, 1915) - No children

First Lady: 1915-1921

Death: December 28, 1961

Place of Burial: Washington Cathedral, Washington, DC

The *Muddy Boots*

*M*odern historians are emphatic about consulting only primary source material, which of course is important. It is also important to note that not all primary sources are completely honest, candid or accurate in their memories, especially those from decades before. First Lady scholars have long realized that Edith Wilson's recollections in *My Memoirs* need to be taken with a lump of salt and considerable fact-checking.

But this is the story that Edith Bolling Galt Wilson, Woodrow Wilson's second wife, tells in her *Memoirs*, written some twenty years after her time as First Lady. It may be somewhat massaged. It may be a few odd recollections cobbled together. It may even be made up of whole cloth. But it still is a terrific *story*, and one that should be told anyway.

Edith Meets the President

Edith Bolling Galt, a forty-two-year-old Virginia-born widow, had lived in Washington for nearly two decades, but her social circle was far removed from the political arena.

In early 1915, she became friendly with Helen Bones, Woodrow Wilson's cousin, who had been invited by the grieving President to move into the White House to handle his domestic and social responsibilities after his wife's death. Miss Bones and Mrs. Galt were close in age, and had common interests. One afternoon, while they were out-and-about, they were caught in a rainstorm not far from the Executive Mansion. Helen suggested that Edith might like to come for tea in the family quarters, but Edith was hesitant. According to her memoirs, she was concerned that her muddy boots would soil the White House carpets.

Assured by Helen that muddy boots would not be a problem, the two women, wet and chilled, went inside and as they approached the private elevator, met none other than President Wilson and his physician, Dr. Cary Grayson. The men had been golfing and were caught in the same downpour. They invited themselves to the ladies' tea party, and the rest would be history.

So far so good, and a nice story, according to Mrs. Galt.

But the real muddy part was the story behind that first meeting. It may have been a very discreet fix-up, certainly unbeknownst to the President, and perhaps to Edith as well.

It was Dr. Cary Grayson who had introduced Helen Bones to Edith Galt in the first place. He realized that Helen Bones, with no friends in Washington save a despondent president, might be in need of a companion herself, so the match was made between Miss Bones and Mrs. Galt, and the women got on well.

Grayson was a Navy doctor a score of years younger than President Wilson, and was courting a young woman named Altrude Gordon. Miss Gordon's deceased parents had been close friends of the Widow Galt, who then became a close friend and surrogate mother-figure to the object of Cary Grayson's affections. Altrude, by the way, was somewhat cool to the doctor's attentions, but Edith liked him and encouraged the match. She was also aware that Dr. Grayson was the personal physician to President Wilson. That was as close as she had ever come to anything resembling political circles.

Again, so far so good. And absolutely true.

Dr. Grayson had devotedly nursed the late Ellen Wilson through the last few months of her life. He had become very close to both Wilsons, and knew the sincere depth of their loving thirty-year marriage. The first Mrs. Wilson, a prescient and insightful woman, had always been aware of Woodrow's dependence on a woman's nurturing attentions. She also knew she was dying, and that Woodrow would suffer unbearably once that happened. Wilson was not told of his wife's inevitable fate until near the end. She made a deathbed request to Dr. Grayson to "take care of Woodrow." Grayson would honor that request.

As expected, Wilson plummeted into a deep depression when his wife died. His personal grief was compounded by the monumental stress of a terrible war about to explode in Europe just as Ellen Wilson was being laid to rest.

Grief and mourning must run its course, President or not. Wilson couldn't eat, lost weight, was plagued by insomnia, found it hard to concentrate, and his stress-induced headaches and digestive problems resurfaced. Dr. Grayson prescribed a bland diet, regular exercise and fresh air, which he believed would help Wilson sleep. To make sure his patient got that fresh air and exercise, Dr. Grayson became his golfing buddy.

The Fix-Up?

So, did Dr. Grayson plan the meeting between Woodrow Wilson and Edith Galt? He knew them both, and was in a perfect position to make introductions. He obviously could *not* have known they would all be caught in the rain. But then again, he easily could have suggested tea at the White House to Helen Bones—rain or shine.

A chance meeting at the elevator would have required some very elaborate choreography, especially with no modern conveniences to coordinate such chance. Then again, it could easily have been pre-arranged for the four people to meet in the private quarters for tea at a particular time. The President and his doctor could have crashed the tea party very conveniently and innocently enough. Or not.

For certain, Woodrow Wilson knew nothing about a meeting ploy, even if there was one. He had loved his first wife deeply, and was not seeking new romance. Or so he thought. Miss Bones never admitted to any foreknowledge, and the momentous tea party was a complete surprise to Edith—or so she always said.

Her comments always require a serious investigation. Edith's version of the tale seems to be the only one of this nature. She never mentioned a "chance meeting with muddy boots" to any of her close-knit family at the time. Dr. Grayson never mentioned it. Nor did Ike Hoover, the White House Chief Usher, whose own memoirs provide historians with wonderful insights, and who surely would have known of such an event, especially since he was one of the very few staff members who was aware of the Wilsons' courtship.

The likelihood that this is one of those whole-cloth incidents, like George Washington's cherry tree, is fairly high, especially considering Edith Wilson's inclination and ability to do her own spin-doctoring. But it is also a far more interesting story than any true but mundane facts. A sitting president meeting a potential new First Lady surely deserves a memorable introduction.

The Outcome

But if there *was* a tea party, it was the most successful one since the one in Boston one hundred forty years earlier. Edith also went on to comment that if Woodrow Wilson had been depressed, one would never have known it that afternoon. She said the President was delightful and engaging, with a witty sense of humor. At his best, Woodrow Wilson could definitely be delightful and engaging, with a witty sense of humor. We can trust Edith on that.

Woodrow Wilson had once fallen in love at first sight with Ellen Axson, and he pursued her ardently. It would be habit-forming. He now fell in love with Edith Galt the day they met (however they met), and he pursued *her* in an equally ardent courtship. Eight months later they were married.

And Dr. Cary Grayson *did* marry Altrude Gordon after Woodrow Wilson married Edith Galt.

$\mathcal{E}$dith in $\mathcal{U}$niform

$\mathcal{E}$dith Bolling Galt Wilson was a snappy dresser from the start. At five-foot-nine, she was statuesque and had a sense of style and fashion. When she married Norman Galt, a wealthy Washington jeweler, she had the money to indulge her tastes. She was wearing Charles Frederick Worth gowns long before Woodrow Wilson was on her horizon. Worth, by the way, was one of the most exclusive Paris couturiers, whose design house had been around since the days of the Empress Eugenie a half-century earlier.

Once the Widow Galt married President Woodrow Wilson, she continued to dress with taste befitting a First Lady, and made sure that her President-husband was snappily dressed as well. For the first two years of their marriage, they entertained graciously and frequently. They were inseparable. They went to the theatre, to baseball games, on frequent carriage rides. Edith would always be impeccably dressed, usually sporting her trademark *cartwheel* hat, and dripping orchids, her flower of choice.

The Great War Begins

World War I, called the Great War in those days, had been raging in Europe for more than three years before America entered the fight. Wilson had tried his best to avoid it, but it was inevitable. Edith dutifully turned her style and energies toward the war effort. Her visibility as First Lady made her support essential to the home front. She purchased a small flock of sheep to graze on the White House lawn, thus freeing the gardeners for more important duties. When the sheep were shorn, she had a pound of their wool sent to each state to be auctioned off for war bonds. When *wheatless* and *meatless* and *heatless* days were imposed to conserve food for America's army and allies, she not only complied strictly, but made sure White House compliance was well reported and publicized.

But perhaps most importantly, she joined the Red Cross and proudly wore their uniform. That uniform was not only a symbol of participation in Red Cross efforts, but it gave the women who joined a sense of being useful. It also leveled the playing field, as it were, since women of all walks of life were welcome to participate.

The Red Cross Uniform

Red Cross uniforms of that period were not uniform, however. Designs varied from chapter to chapter, from state to state. Some sources said that Edith had a dusty blue and white striped uniform. It had long sleeves, and a skirt length reaching the top of her shoes. Her hat was a dark blue, with a Red Cross emblem on the band.

Some Red Cross uniforms included a man-tailored suit jacket, but most of the working uniforms featured a long white pinafore-type apron with a Red Cross embroidered on the bib. Its main purpose was to protect the volunteer's personal clothing. Sometimes, if the design featured a shirtwaist or jacket, there was a Red Cross embroidered on a sleeve. Some of the shirtwaist-styles featured a white collar, some a white insert, and some were just plain blue. Sometimes the Red Cross itself was small; sometimes it was very prominent. Occasionally, a navy blue cape was included in the uniform, but the more complete garb was usually reserved for full-time workers, rather than the volunteers.

The Red Cross uniform caps also ran a gamut, and hats of some sort were still essential. Some were sturdy framed hats with wide brims. Some were white caps similar to those worn by nurses. Occasionally, there were wimple-style caps that hung low in the back, similar to an Arabian headdress.

The duties of Red Cross volunteer Mrs. Wilson were moderate and flexible. It is said that she sewed pajamas for the wounded. Her sewing machine was one of the few personal possessions she brought with her to the White House. She occasionally played hostess at the Red Cross canteens at various railroad stations for soldiers passing through Washington to or from deployment. On at least one occasion she went to Washington's Union Station to pour coffee and distribute sandwiches at a canteen run by First-Lady-to-be Eleanor Roosevelt.

Edith Wilson was an attractive woman, and a photogenic one. She knew it. She was also savvy to the power of the press and its photographers, and happy to oblige with a picture from time to time. When a photograph of the First Lady wearing her Red Cross uniform was featured in the newspapers, it is said that thousands of women rushed to volunteer their services. Another First-Lady-to-be, Grace Coolidge, was one of them.

First Ladies always have influence.

ℒalique ℬrooch

The Lady

𝒩orman Galt, Edith's wealthy first husband, had been the owner of a prestigious Washington jewelry establishment that had existed for decades. Thomas Jefferson had purchased from them. Mary Lincoln had been a customer. Obviously, whatever Edith wanted in the way of jewelry was available and accessible. When Norman died, Edith, a stylish woman whose statuesque frame did justice to a dramatic sense of fashion, was very well provided for.

By the time she married Woodrow Wilson, the President was also financially comfortable, perhaps for the first time in his life. During his thirty-year marriage to Ellen Axson, he had struggled to support a growing family and a seemingly endless revolving door of family house guests. By 1915, his three daughters were grown and no longer needed his financial support. His personal housing and accouterments were gratis the country. Ditto transportation, medical care and golfing privileges. The only thing that made a serious dent in his annual salary was the expense of feeding and entertaining guests. (A federal budget for such purposes would not be instituted until the Coolidge administration a decade later.)

Thus the *new* Mrs. Wilson was in a position to treat herself very generously, which she always did.

The Brooch

René Lalique (1860-1945) was a French designer of extraordinary jewelry, glass and related art nouveau decorative objects. By World War I, his reputation for superb artistry and craftsmanship was equal to that of Louis Comfort Tiffany.

One of his specialty creations had been a large brooch. It featured eight pale green-gray pigeons artistically perched on a gold tree branch. It was an oversized piece, about six inches across, much too imposing for most women to wear at the shoulder, the neck or breast, the common positions for a brooch. Perhaps because of its size or price tag, the pin was never sold or reproduced, and it remained in Lalique's personal collection for a long time.

The Lady, The Brooch and The Great War

The first war had been called The Great War, to encompass its size, its armies, its scope, its breadth and its cost in fortune and most importantly, its casualty list. It began in Europe in 1914, but it took three years before President Wilson was finally forced by circumstances to commit the United States to keeping the world safe for democracy. Once America was committed and soldiers deployed, hostilities ended within the year. It was 1918, and Europe, aflame for four years, was exhausted.

Four empires were toppled forever: the young, bellicose and pretentious German Empire, the thoroughly rotted Ottoman (Turkish) Empire, the semi-decadent Austria-Hungarian Empire and the totally decadent and inwardly seething Russian Empire that imploded into its own revolution even before the war ended. The British Empire survived, just barely.

In short, the world was a mess.

President Wilson decided to personally lead the U.S. peace delegation at the peace talks in Paris, aimed at restructuring a new world order and a new map of Europe. Naturally, he brought Mrs. Wilson along. They were still honeymooners.

Paris, and indeed most of Europe, hailed President *Weelson* as their savior, and the American First Couple was lavishly feted and entertained. They were paraded and photographed. They were honored and gifted.

The French were extravagant in their hospitality and generosity, and designed a magnificent Medal of Honor for the American President. Then, in a stroke of marketing and advertising genius, René Lalique rediscovered the large brooch that had been tucked away in his safe for some time. Declaring the pigeons to be *doves* and the tree branch rechristened an *olive branch*, the pin was renamed the *Peace Brooch*. Perhaps also deciding that Edith Wilson's imposing figure would enhance the large bauble, it was presented to Mrs. Wilson, the jeweler's widow, who was delighted by the completely unexpected gift, and certainly appreciated its craftsmanship and value.

The Lady and the Brooch After-Story

It is not certain whether Edith Wilson ever had many opportunities to wear her Lalique Peace Brooch in Paris, or indeed during the next few years. Overtaxed by the stress and strain of a complicated and acrimonious peace conference and the subsequent recalcitrant American Congress that declined to accept the treaty their President had signed, Wilson collapsed from a massive stroke only a few months later. Formal entertaining at the White House ceased.

In 1920, however, the official White House portrait of the second Mrs. Wilson was commissioned and painted by Seymour M. Stone, a Russian-born artist. Still regal and youthful looking at forty-eight, the ever-stylish First Lady was depicted seated, wearing an elegant black and white gown. The bodice, draped in fashionable folds, was very much in keeping with the popular new styles of the burgeoning 1920s.

And there, affixed to her right *hip*, where the folds met, was the Lalique Peace Brooch. The large ornament was perfectly placed, doing honor to the lady, the brooch, and the savvy of René Lalique, who knew instinctively that his doves had found their way to a permanent home.

The portrait hangs prominently and permanently in the Woodrow Wilson House in Washington.

FLORENCE MABEL KLING DeWOLFE HARDING

Born; August 15, 1860

Place of Birth: Marion, OH

Parents: Amos H. Kling; Louisa Bouton Kling

Marriage: (1) Henry DeWolfe (div.) - 1 son, Marshall Eugene De Wolfe

(2) Warren G. Harding: July 8, 1891 - No children

First Lady: 1921-1923

Death: November 21, 1924

Place of Burial: Harding Memorial, Marion, OH

Thick Veils and a Velvet Collar

Midwestern Wife

Florence Kling Harding, nicknamed "Duchess" by her husband partly due to her imperious ways, wasn't a bad-looking woman but was certainly no beauty. Some people unkindly assumed she might have been Warren Harding's mother. Five years older than her definitely handsome husband, she had already been married, had a child and was divorced by the time they met. Most people did *not* know that Florence was a very sick woman.

By the time she was in her mid-thirties, she had developed a chronic and serious kidney ailment that sometimes kept her bedridden for weeks. By 1900, one of her kidneys had already been removed. Since modern antibiotics and treatments had not yet been developed, there were times when her death was considered imminent. As might be expected, illness takes its toll on all parts of the body. Florence showed her years, and they weren't kind.

The Duchess had a decent enough medium-build figure. The thick ankles one sometimes sees in her full-length photographs as First Lady in the early 1920s when hemlines had risen a few inches were the result of her failing kidneys, not from overweight. She was also nearsighted, and wore a fashionable pince-nez, but avoided wearing it for the camera whenever possible. Her biggest cosmetic problem was her sagging skin.

Warren Harding, on the other hand, looked like the classic matinee idol of the 1920s: Six feet tall, with a fashionable—but not huge—paunch. His shock of white wavy hair contrasted dramatically with his swarthy complexion, and belied the fact that he was only fifty-five when he was elected president. Most people considered him the best-looking president since Franklin Pierce in 1853, and by that time, nobody remembered Pierce.

Perhaps due to Florence's poor health, the Hardings had no children together, but the *Marion Star*, the newspaper they owned in Ohio, had become very successful, especially under the Duchess' watchful eye on the circulation department and the books. While they were by no means wealthy, they were definitely comfortable, and Florence could indulge her vanities—and she was unquestionably vain. She brought style and curls to her graying hair by having her hair regularly marcelled, the new look of the early twentieth century. She never bothered to dye her hair, perhaps because Warren Harding's handsomely white hair was wildly becoming to him. But she bought every cream and powder and lotion and potion that promised the Fountain of Youth. In desperation, Florence took to wearing hats with thick, dark veils or veils with polka-dot accents to disguise the wrinkles that refused to disappear, no matter what the container said.

Senate Wife

The twenty years Florence spent as Mrs. Harding of Marion, Ohio had never been happy for her. She had few if any close friends. Her husband was a chronic philanderer, partially because of his wife's health, which precluded intimacy, and partially due to her domineering personality, which also precluded intimacy. Running the *Marion Star* and their shared interest in politics seemed to be their only strong bond.

When Warren Harding was elected to the U.S. Senate in 1914, a thrilled Florence treated herself to a brand new wardrobe in anticipation of what she hoped would be a wonderful new life for her in Washington. She had never spared expense when it came to her personal appearance and this time was no exception. But the shops and stores of middle-class Ohio were hopelessly Midwestern by Washington fashion standards, and the poor Duchess, now in her mid-fifties, was considered not only old, but dowdy and *outré*. She didn't fit. She left her calling cards everywhere, but her calls were unreturned. Invitations were few, and those were only to the large receptions where *everyone* was invited. Once again, she had no friends. Hurt and angered by the rebuff, she kept a little red notebook full of names of all those who snubbed her just in case retribution might be an option.

Then, to add injury to the insult, she had another bout with her remaining and chronically blocked kidney that laid her up for months. Once again, her death was expected.

It was about this time that Florence Harding received a great gift: the sincere friendship of Washington socialite Evalyn Walsh McLean. The two women had become casually acquainted, but pleasantly enough for the kind-hearted Evalyn to pay a visit to her sick friend.

They were an odd couple by most accounts. Florence was twenty-five years older than Evalyn, who was arguably the wealthiest woman in Washington, if not the country. She owned the Hope Diamond. She was also glamorous, socially prominent and popular. All things Florence was not. Evalyn's husband, Ned McLean, was even wealthier. He owned the *Washington Post*, among other publications.

Despite their obvious differences, Florence and Evalyn forged a close bond, perhaps in part because their respective husbands were of the good-ol'-boy school: hard drinking, cigar-smoking, poker-playing and unrepentant chippie-chasers. The men became great pals, and it frequently became a foursome, with the Hardings as regular guests at the McLean estate in Georgetown.

Trademark Velvet Neckband

Evalyn took a fashion-hand with the Duchess, her new best friend in sore need of a make-over. She introduced her to a more stylish hairdresser. She helped her choose smarter clothes and hats. She made sure Florence was invited to all the best parties. For the first time in perhaps ever, Florence Harding was socially important. And happy.

And it was Evalyn who suggested to Warren Harding that he purchase a gift for his wife, once she had recovered. She helped him choose a beautiful cameo brooch that could be affixed to a black velvet choker collar, a style that had been popularized by Queen Alexandra, the wife of Edward VII. The stylish Queen had a scar on her neck that she wanted to keep hidden, and the velvet and/or jeweled neck collars were designed to protect the Queen's secret. It made a huge fashion statement in the early twentieth century. Every woman was wearing one.

For Christmas following his election in November, 1920, Warren Harding purchased a large diamond sunburst for his long-suffering wife. It could also be fastened to her velvet collar. It is said that Evalyn had selected it for him as well. It was *trés chic*. She had excellent taste.

It became the Duchess' trademark accessory as First Lady, and the one she cherished the most. Whether she loved it to celebrate becoming First Lady, because her husband bought it for her, or because her dear friend chose it, or because it was a piece of truly knockout jewelry, it doesn't matter.

The important thing was that it concealed her sagging neck, and she wore it for the rest of her life, which, sadly enough was not destined to be very long. Both Hardings would die before their natural term in office ended.

$\mathcal{G}$RACE $\mathcal{A}$NNA $\mathcal{G}$OODHUE $\mathcal{C}$OOLIDGE

Date of Birth: January 3, 1879

Place of Birth: Burlington, VT

Parents: Andrew I. Goodhue; Lemira Barnett Goodhue

Marriage: October 4, 1905

Children: John Coolidge, Calvin Coolidge, Jr. (d. age 16)

First Lady: 1923-1929

Date of Death: July 8, 1957

Place of Burial: Plymouth Notch Cemetery, Plymouth Notch, VT

Hat, Purse and Thwarted Jodhpurs

From the beginning of First Ladyhood, and probably long before, no lady, First or otherwise, would be seen outside her home without her hat, her purse and her gloves. Most middle-class women had several hats, purses and pairs of gloves. Even women in the lower-income classes had a Sunday hat, purse and pair of gloves. It was as essential to their appearance as a pair of shoes. Grace Coolidge had dozens of hats, many of which had been specifically purchased by her husband who always took a particular interest in his wife's wardrobe.

Speaking of *pairs*, the Coolidges were an unlikely pair. Grace Goodhue Coolidge was warm and outgoing, with scores of friends that she maintained for life. Calvin Coolidge, on the other hand, was an odd fish socially, difficult to warm to and silent as a clam. Even Grace's parents tried to dissuade their only daughter from such a bland choice. Still, their marriage of nearly thirty years was a genuinely happy one, supported largely by their wry and engaging senses of humor. His was dry as peanut butter on rye toast; hers was teasing and mimicking. It worked for them. She always claimed that he made her laugh.

Many years after living in the White House, a young female reporter asked the Widow Grace about her *romance* with Calvin Coolidge. Mrs. C. looked incredulously at the young woman and asked, "Did you ever meet my husband?"

The marriage was not an equal partnership, however. Not even close. Calvin Coolidge was as sexist a husband as ever occupied the White House, although he truly adored his pretty and personable wife. If he behaved disrespectfully to her, which today would be unquestioned, it was totally unconscious and unintended on his part. He would likely be crushed to think he might have hurt her feelings. It never occurred to him.

Calvin Coolidge, the New England Puritan, absolutely believed it was a man's world, and a woman's place was not only in the home, but in a supporting role in that same home. Chez Coolidge, *he* was the undisputed master of the house, and Grace's role was contained within the sphere he deemed appropriate for *his* wife. Politics of course, was not included in that sphere. When he cut their honeymoon short in order to make a campaign speech for a place on the Northampton, Massachusetts school board, she didn't even know he was running. Years later, when he ran for Lieutenant Governor of Massachusetts, she didn't know he was running then, either. It was not that he wished to ignore her. It was merely that his political activities did not affect her. His job might change, but hers remained the same: Mrs. Coolidge, housewife.

Coolidge believed that not only was politics a man's business, but *all* business was a man's business. If Mrs. Coolidge, housewife, objected to the limitations of her world she never complained, at least not openly. But as a needlewoman who sewed, knitted and crocheted with fair skill, she once quipped that you could tell when she was upset by how hard she worked those needles. It was simply not her way to generate arguments she could never win.

It wasn't until Calvin Coolidge became Lieutenant Governor of Massachusetts that he began to realize the political asset he had in his attractive spouse. By the end of World War I, women had become more and more active in a man's world, and Mrs. C. could hold her own very nicely. She was a graduate of the University of Vermont, a teacher of the deaf, and a huge baseball fan. She was familiar with all the latest moving pictures, novels, magazine stories and popular songs. She was good looking, stylish, possessed of an impish good humor and a wall-to-wall smile, a terrific benefit that Calvin began to discover, much to his surprise. He faded into the woodwork, but people always seemed to remember the delightful *Mrs.* Coolidge.

The "Capital" Coolidges

When Calvin Coolidge became Vice President, and later President in 1923 following the death of President Harding, he enjoyed taking his wife to many of the functions he was obliged to attend. The 1920s were a boom-time of grand-scale pop culture as we have come to know it. Vice President Coolidge was in constant demand, particularly once people had a taste of his devastatingly dry humor. The couple was at the top of the A-list of guests of honor, and they dined out four or even five times a week. "Gotta eat somewhere," Coolidge remarked. Hosts knew better than to expect a speech from "Silent Cal," but they did expect an appearance and a photo-op, and maybe even a memorable quip. The amazingly popular Coolidge obliged.

Mrs. Coolidge, with her innate warmth, easy charm and stylish appearance, was just as popular. The two of them were invited everywhere.

Grace's Pants and Accessories

First Lady Coolidge was not without her own social obligations. She hosted teas, luncheons, visitors, and handled volumes of correspondence—the usual First Lady drill. If her husband wanted her company on one of his out-and-abouts, she was plucked from the midst of her busyness at the last minute. The extent of her participation, however, was to smile, to accept a bouquet, kiss a baby and perhaps say "thank you." Still, she required a large and fashionable wardrobe. And her husband, who always took a remarkably close interest in said wardrobe, was happy to have his wife looking snappy and tasteful. He was a thrifty man by nature but never skimped when it came to his wife's clothing. In his own way, he was very proud of her.

But the new First Lady had thought that a little exercise might do her good, and decided to take up horseback riding instead of her daily hour-long walk. She signed up for lessons and purchased an attractive riding outfit complete with a hat, riding jacket and fashionable jodhpurs—riding pants, diamond-shaped in the seat, and tight fitting in the leg. When the President saw his wife modeling her new outfit, he was not pleased. Women, and especially First Ladies, did not wear trousers. Period. The unabashedly sexist man cautioned, "I think you will get along at this job fully as well if you do not try anything new." So Grace returned the jodhpurs, cancelled her classes, and continued her daily walks—in a dress.

Calvin Coolidge would likely be devastated that people today consider him unbearably dismissive to his wife. He never meant disrespect. He loved her dearly, and she knew it. It was merely that he could not fathom that any need *she* had other than her health might be just as important as his immediate concerns, presidential or not, whatever they were.

But she once asked innocently enough, if she might be given a copy of the President's daily schedule to know if and when she was needed and plan accordingly. Coolidge tersely replied. "That information isn't given out indiscriminately, Grace." So from then on, she kept the hat and purse and gloves that matched her daily outfit on a conveniently located table. Whenever she was summoned, she would be ready at a moment's notice. If Grace ever had a mind to set his attitudes straight, it is unknown. It is also unlikely. The only thing that is known is that Mrs. Coolidge remained just as silent on the subject as Silent Cal.

Some people fight; others adapt.

The *R*ed *D*ress

*H*oward Chandler Christy was a well-known illustrator, artist and portrait painter during the early part of the twentieth century. When he was commissioned to paint the official White House portrait of Grace Coolidge in the 1920s, he became famous. That portrait is arguably his most popular work, and it immortalized an otherwise forgotten First Lady.

All portrait artists strive for more than just likeness. A photographer can do that. An artist's aim is to paint the inner person as well, the invisible person within, whether it is their kindness, or wisdom, or sorrow, or strength. Christy spent a great deal of time with Mrs. Coolidge to reach the soul of a woman known only for her ear-to-ear smile and her reluctance to speak publicly.

The truth behind Mrs. C. was that she was intelligent and educated, and possessed of a delightfully sly sense of humor that complemented her husband's dry wit. Everyone who knew her, liked her. She had graduated from the University of Vermont, was a founding member of the Pi Beta Phi Sorority, and was, in today's terminology, a special ed teacher. She taught the deaf.

New England Housewife

When she married and began her family, Grace became a traditional wife and mother, since the uber-sexist Calvin Coolidge would tolerate no less, and she demanded no more. She cooked and baked well enough, did her own housework and cared for their two sons, which included teaching them how to throw and catch and pitch a baseball. She was an avid needlewoman, and found social outlets in church and community activities in their town. The marriage was happy. Calvin loved her dearly, and she knew it. He also became surprisingly proud of his attractive and personable wife. Surprisingly, until he attained enough public stature to "bring the missus" to events, he never gave her considerable social assets a second thought, let alone worthy of political value.

But he did know that he had a good-looking wife, and he wanted her to be well dressed. He was amazingly generous about her wardrobe. And just as amazingly, he was very particular about his own wardrobe. This thoroughly confounded his contemporaries who knew the well-known Coolidge sense of thrift. Coolidge had always loved to go clothes shopping with his wife, and often selected her outfits himself. She claimed he was much pickier than she was. She admitted that she grew tired, and was happy to settle for whatever was handy. Not so Calvin. He pressed for the perfect, especially since Grace had a nice figure and looked good in the styles of the 1920s, at least the ones appropriate to a woman in her mid-forties.

The Portrait Dilemma

The story goes that painter Christy's idea was to portray the First Lady as a woman who was stylish, warm, and possessed of considerable depth, all qualities Grace Coolidge had in abundance. What better way than showing her in a fashionable dress, standing beside Rob Roy, their white collie, but with an uncharacteristic serious expression? Pets always add warmth to an individual, and both Coolidges were passionate animal lovers.

The depth part was the contribution of the insightful artist who, when asked about Mrs. C's unusual absence of broad smile, remarked that he thought he once saw a look of resignation in her face. A wise man, Christy.

The story continues that once the artist had decided on the tone of the portrait, he spent hours searching the First Lady's closet for the perfect dress. She had a very large wardrobe, as do all First Ladies, and Christy had many choices. The President took his usual active interest in Grace's clothing, and suggested a particular white dress which he claimed to be his favorite. Christy disagreed. He had decided on a bright red dress, low-cut but not too low, sleeveless, boyishly slim-lined and draped to the ankle, as was the current fashion. Grace, as usual, had no public comment on the subject, although she was inclined to permit the artist his artistic judgment.

Coolidge strongly pressed his preference for the white gown, and the *President* was not accustomed to being thwarted. Finally Christy diplomatically explained his *artistic* reasoning— the red dress is a brilliant contrast with the white dog. President Coolidge knew nothing about art or artistic temperament or even contrasting color choices, but he did know he was losing that battle. He still persisted, presenting his parting shot: "Dye the dog."

The Prez was overruled.

The portrait of First Lady Grace Coolidge in her knockout red gown, next to the white collie, is arguably the most famous and most widely reproduced of all the formal First Lady portraits.

$\mathcal{L}$ou $\mathcal{H}$ENRY $\mathcal{H}$OOVER

Date of Birth: March 29, 1875

Place of Birth: Waterloo, Iowa

Parents: Charles Delano Henry; Florence Weed Henry

Marriage: February 10, 1899

Children: Herbert Clark Hoover, Jr.; Allan Henry Hoover

First Lady: 1929-1933

Date of Death: January 7, 1944

Burial Place: Herbert Hoover Presidential Site, West Branch, IA

The *Hitching* Skirt

*L*ou Henry Hoover was a child of the West, even though she was born in Iowa. Her parents moved to California when Lou was only nine. With no sons in the family, and her only sister eight years younger, Lou became her father's outdoor companion. She learned to ride expertly, shoot a gun with fair accuracy, fish, hunt, build a fire, climb a tree—rugged tomboy activities. On the other hand, the family was solidly middle-income. Her father was a banker, so she was also exposed to the benefits of town life: art, literature, social culture, and a good education.

Once graduated from high school, Miss Henry, tall, slim and athletic, attended a *normal school*, the term used for a two-year teacher's college. She excelled academically, preferring math and science. Those were the subjects usually reserved for the male teachers. Then again, Miss Henry always bucked the norm.

At twenty, during a summer break, Lou attended a lecture on geology, given by J.C. Branner, a professor at the recently opened Stanford University in Palo Alto. She was enthralled, and asked her parents if she might apply to Stanford and study geology. Her family was amenable. After all, the tuition was free.

All she had to do was pass the entrance examination, which she did easily.

Stanford

In 1895, when Lou Henry entered Stanford, geology was unequivocally a men-only discipline. A lady might audit a lecture or even take a basic course, but women were not expected to pursue it as a career choice any more than they would dream of becoming a railroad engineer.

Also in 1895, when geology student Lou Henry was a young woman of twenty, the fashions had changed dramatically from the earlier hoop skirts and the bustles—particularly out West. Women were more athletic. They rode bicycles. They skated. They bowled. They played tennis and golf. A split-skirt, sometimes called *skorts* or *culottes* today, was made for riding astride, and was part of every western woman's wardrobe.

Skirts, of course, still trailed the ground, but the voluminous petticoats of yesteryear had disappeared. The trend was a slimming A-line style, topped by a shirtwaist or man-tailored blouse, and frequently an attractive jacket. Laces and ruffles were still there, but reserved for evenings. Daytime was for moving around.

As expected, the geology class at Stanford was male with the exception of Miss Henry. To say her presence did not generate enthusiasm amongst her classmates was an understatement. When her high grades proved her worth academically, she was tolerated, but the fellows smirked that in the field exercises she would be left in the dust. Literally.

They did not have long to wait. Rocks do not grow indoors, or in the middle of town. Field trips to rugged terrain are an integral part of the coursework, and soon enough an outdoor lesson was scheduled. Miss Henry, long-skirted and sensibly mid-heeled, was included, amid grumbling that she would not be able to keep up with the guys. She kept up very nicely. The story continues that the students arrived at an area that a local farmer had fenced off for his cattle. Most of the guys bounded the fence easily, but a few of the more chivalrous gentlemen remained behind to assist their female classmate, offering a hand to help her over.

Lou Henry smiled at them, hitched her skirt to mid-calf, put one hand on the top rail, and leapt over in a graceful bound. It was obviously something she had done many times growing up. She did not need their hand, or a leg up, either. She could hold her own very well, both scholastically and in the field. She would become one of Stanford's first female graduates, and the very first American woman to earn a degree in geology.

Then she met Herbert Hoover, another geology student. They were introduced by none other than Professor Branner, whose lecture had so entranced her. Consciously or unconsciously, she decided to switch her plans a bit, and *major* in Herbert Hoover. Immediately after her graduation, they married and embarked on a very active and fascinating life. A few years into their marriage, she would co-author a translation of a Renaissance treatise on mining, written in Latin, no less, which won her accolades in geological circles.

$\mathscr{L}$ou $\mathscr{H}$oover's $\mathscr{U}$niform

$\mathscr{L}$ou Henry Hoover is one of the least known First Ladies of the twentieth century, possibly for no other reason than her own abhorrence of courting publicity.

During World War I, when Eleanor Roosevelt ran a canteen serving donuts to doughboys, and First Lady Edith Wilson occasionally showed up for a photo-op, Lou Henry Hoover was criss-crossing the Atlantic, writing articles and making public speeches throughout the U.S. to raise awareness and money for starving Belgium, which was being decimated by the advancing Germans. Humanitarianism on a grand scale would become as much a part of Mrs. Hoover's life as it was her husband's.

Lou Henry was not born rich. She came from a middle-class family, raised in California in the 1880s when it was still the Wild West. When she married Herbert Hoover, he was akin to one of Horatio Alger's poster boys—the poor boy who makes good through dint of his own talents and efforts. With Hoover, it was makes good big time. In 1900 he was twenty-five, and already earing $45,000 per year as a mining engineer—at least ten times that amount today, or maybe more. As a point of comparison, the President of the United States made only $50,000 a year in 1900.

When the Hoovers married in 1899, they immediately went to China where Herbert had been engaged to supervise a huge mining project. Their married life began with six servants, according to traditional Chinese custom-for-foreigners. A dozen years later the Hoovers, now with two young sons, were living in the fashionable Mayfair section of London with even more servants. Hoover had become a millionaire several times over.

Herbert Hoover was one of our wealthiest presidents—all of his own earning. There was no inheritance, no family pedigree, no fortuitous marriage dowry. In 1929, when they entered the White House in their mid-fifties, the Hoovers had become one of the best known couples in the country—but it was not from mining engineering. He had become a mega-humanitarian, with a genius for administration proven by his overseas volunteer war-relief assistance in Europe. Mrs. Hoover had embraced that activist life as well, but in her own way and on her own terms. One aspect of those terms was her disinclination for *personal* publicity. For the *cause,* yes; for herself, never.

A Person of Substance

Mrs. Hoover could have purchased her gowns and dresses from the most expensive designers and merchants in the world, but while her wardrobe always consisted of well-made clothing of fine quality and she was considered a well-dressed woman, she was generally indifferent to fashion. She wore sensible shoes. She was a large woman, but not fat: the slim, athletic figure of her youth had matured with age. She was what Harry Truman would later say about his own wife: "exactly what a woman her age *should* look like." Like Martha Washington a century and a half earlier, she would always be appropriate for the occasion, but she was not particularly stylish, nor did she care. By the 1920s, the emerging movie stars and theatrical personalities were the fashion setters, not a fifty-year-old wife of the Secretary of Commerce.

What Lou Hoover *did* care about, however, was the Girl Scouts. She had learned about the organization in London, where it was called the Girl Guides. When the Hoovers were asked by President Wilson to return to the U.S. in 1918, Lou became seriously interested in the Girl Guides' fledgling American counterpart, believing that her own Western upbringing was a perfect match between person and organization. With no daughters of her own, she nevertheless volunteered to help young girls combine traditional domestic duties with the outdoors and nature and community activism. She quickly rose in the leadership ranks.

Scout Leader

By 1921, Lou Hoover had risen to become first vice president on the national Board of Directors of the Girl Scouts of America (GSA), and during her years of active involvement, enrollment would rise nearly a hundredfold by the time of her death in 1944.

Between 1922 and 1928, Mrs. Hoover served as the national president of the Girl Scouts. It was not in name only. If her name was to be on the letterhead, it was because she earned it.

First Ladies, starting with Edith Wilson, were, and still are, invited to become Honorary Girl Scout president. Lou was not *honorary*. She was its *working* president. She spent long hours planning the general focus and goals, the programs and activities, and even offering suggestions for merit badge qualifications. She logged thousands of miles over the years to meet and interact with regional officers, troop leaders and many hundreds of Girls Scouts themselves.

She is quoted as saying, "To me, the outing part of scouting has always been the most important. The happiest part of my own very happy childhood and girlhood was without doubt the hours and days, sometimes entire months, which I spent in pseudo-pioneering or scouting in our wonderful western mountains with my father in our vacation times. So I cannot but want every girl to have the same widening, simplifying, joy-getting influences in her own life." Thus, in addition to her GSA presidential duties, she personally started local Girl Scout troops in both Washington and in Palo Alto, CA, where the Hoovers maintained their private home. She even served as the Washington troop's Scout Leader.

Like her husband, Mrs. Hoover declined any salary or compensation for any of her public activities. She was also quick to provide substantial personal funds to spearhead other projects she believed were important. It was never made public.

The Favorite Outfit

Mrs. Hoover also took a hand in helping design the Girl Scout uniform, which would be re-adapted periodically, but one that basically continued for many years. It was always green.

Troop leader uniforms were also green, but styled for a mature woman. They were also not uniform. They varied. Sometimes they were a muted-green shirtwaist style dress with a dark green velvet or corduroy collar. Sometimes they were green skirts with a white blouse and green jacket. Occasionally the styles were belted. Sometimes there was a matching full-length green coat. Frequently there was a dark green bandanna or necktie.

A dark green hat, of course, was essential. No outfit was complete without a hat in those days! While the hat design varied over the years, and sometimes changed from region to region or chapter to chapter, Lou's hat was usually wide-brimmed, and always affixed with the Girl Scout emblem.

Lou Hoover was still on the Girl Scouts' national board of directors with substantive responsibilities when she became First Lady. She could not neglect her many White House functions, but she also was not about to neglect those administrative duties she had undertaken of her own accord and had enjoyed for nearly a decade. She hired, at her own expense, a secretary exclusively devoted to Girl Scout matters. She hosted many of their executive meetings in White House conference rooms, and high-level Girl Scout executives were occasionally invited to the Hoovers' private getaway cabin Lou had built in the Maryland mountains.

Lou Henry Hoover was not as widely photographed as her predecessor, Grace Coolidge, or her successor, Eleanor Roosevelt. Like Edith Roosevelt, she shunned the camera. Most people today would not be able to identify her image. In the few formal photographs that exist of her, she looked more like a wealthy society matron (which she was) than an athletic Western-bred activist— which she also was.

There are however, several photographs, and even some movie footage of Mrs. H. in her Girl Scout leader uniform. It is said that those photos were her favorites.

*A*NNA *E*LEANOR *R*OOSEVELT *R*OOSEVELT

Date of Birth: October 11, 1884

Place of Birth: New York, NY

Parents: Elliott Roosevelt; Anna Livingston Hall Roosevelt

Marriage: March 17, 1905

Children: Anna Eleanor Roosevelt Dall Boettiger Halsted; James

Roosevelt; Elliott Roosevelt; Franklin Delano Roosevelt, Jr.;

John Aspinwall Roosevelt

First Lady: 1933-1945

Date of Death: November 7, 1962

Burial Place: Hyde Park, NY

The $\mathcal{B}$ad $\mathcal{D}$ress $\mathcal{S}$tory

$\mathcal{T}$here have been a few First Ladies who were poor. A few were orphaned early in life. Some had memories of a sad childhood. Few, however, could equal the emptiness of Eleanor Roosevelt's early years. The only saving grace was that she was not poor.

Anna Eleanor Roosevelt was *born* a Roosevelt, the *Anna* part dropped from the start. Her mother, Anna Hall, was a beautiful New York socialite who died when Eleanor was eight. Her father, Elliott, was Theodore Roosevelt's younger brother. Despite his patrician background and genuine charm, he had become an alcoholic and opiate addict by his mid-twenties. Some claim it was to offset pain from a riding accident; some modern scholars suggest that he may have suffered pain from a brain tumor. Whatever the reasons, Elliott was unfit to live within the family circle, and saw the daughter he dearly loved only intermittently. He died when he was thirty-four. Eleanor was ten.

Uncle Theodore and his two sisters always took a benevolent interest in their young niece, but Eleanor went to live permanently with her Grandmother Hall, a somewhat dotty old lady, and an assortment of equally dotty—and flagrantly dissipated—Hall aunts and uncles who still lived at home. It was a loveless and lonely childhood.

Eleanor did *not* look at all like her mother. She looked exactly like the Roosevelts. Nor did she have the effortless social graces of both her parents. Not unsurprisingly, Eleanor grew up withdrawn and painfully shy. She was a very tall girl, eventually reaching five-foot-ten, extremely thin, unathletic and awkward, with a hopeless overbite and few friends or opportunities to improve her loneliness.

The Halls were wealthy, with a large estate along the Hudson River as well as a town house in New York City, but they were definitely peculiar. It must be chalked up to Grandma Hall's eccentricities that Eleanor was always oddly dressed. Contemporary sources indicate that even as a schoolgirl, she wore dresses that had gone out of fashion years earlier. Most likely, these were the navy-and-white sailor-style outfits popular during the post-Civil War era. The style remained popular for many years, although by the 1890s, when Eleanor was growing up, those fashions had definitely changed.

There is a story that when she was around fourteen, Eleanor attended a Roosevelt family party. Having reached near-full height, she was practically an adult, and obviously ready for woman-fashions of the late 1890s, with their A-lined skirts and tailored shirtwaists. Such styles would have been not only appropriate, but rather becoming, even for a fourteen-year-old.

But to her embarrassment, Eleanor went to the party still dressed as a child, like a somewhat larger version of a ten-year-old rather than as a budding young woman. She was helpless to do anything about it other than to self-consciously try to disappear into thin air.

Perhaps Theodore's daughter Alice attended that same gathering. Perhaps not. The two girl cousins were only a few months apart in age and had known each other from birth. There any resemblance ceased. Not quite as tall as Eleanor, Alice was pretty where Eleanor was homely, graceful where Eleanor was awkward, and extroverted and socially self-assured where Eleanor was insecure and timid. The obvious comparisons were not likely to help Eleanor's lack of confidence.

It might have been that episode that encouraged Theodore's sister, Eleanor's Aunt Anna Roosevelt Cowles, to suggest that her niece be sent to the Allenswood School near London to finish her education. She went, and it became a seminal experience that she would never forget.

Eleanor Roosevelt's misadventures with childhood fashion may or may not have contributed to her eventual disinterest in style as she matured. Her clothing would always be well-tailored from quality fabrics, but like the remarkable woman she became, her wardrobe was invariably designed for usefulness rather than show.

It is said that another Roosevelt cousin attended that party. A distant male cousin two years her senior met her there and remembered her, despite her humiliatingly unstylish dress. He later married her.

$\mathcal{E}$leanor's $\mathcal{U}$niform

$\mathcal{N}$o question about it, the Japanese attack on Pearl Harbor on December 7, 1941 shocked the nation, and everyone rallied to the necessities of war. It was a double blow to First Lady Eleanor Roosevelt. The New Deal and the social changes that it espoused, so dear to her heart, were immediately laid aside as the shift in national priorities went entirely to the war. Not only were her life's efforts put on the sidelines, but in a way, so was she. With no social projects on the front burner, and indeed, interest and funding for all her pet programs quickly fading, what was she going to do with her time and the great influence she had been building for two decades?

It was not enough for Eleanor to merely stop in at a Veterans Administration Hospital now and then, or pour coffee at a canteen like she did during the First War. She wanted to be where she could truly be useful. She begged her husband to allow her to visit the troops overseas. After all, as her polio-stricken husband's eyes and ears, she had logged thousands of air miles visiting mines and prisons and dust-bowl-plagued tenant farms and those planned communities she helped create and so dearly loved. President Franklin Delano Roosevelt pondered the matter, and ran it by his top military advisors. They were not encouraging. War being war, they could not guarantee Mrs. Roosevelt's safety, let alone her conveniences. They would need to spend precious resources and time protecting her, transporting her, and trying to foresee a myriad of unforeseen situations that would make everyone uncomfortable. In short, she would be in the way.

Eleanor was apprised of the adverse reactions, all of which had validity. But she still begged to go. FDR approved, and since he was Commander-in-Chief, she went. And she went wearing the uniform of the American Red Cross. It had changed considerably since Edith Wilson's time twenty-five years earlier. There were no aprons or nurse-like caps and capes. Eleanor wore a nondescript khaki-colored ladies' suit: jacket, skirt and blouse. There was a small Red Cross insignia on the arm. The cap was a square shape, with a broad brim, more like the French army cap of Charles DeGaulle than General MacArthur's. The shoes, of course, were sensible. Never a fashion plate, the almost-dowdy First Lady was now at her best: quintessentially Eleanor.

The First Lady on the Front Lines

Within days of her arrival in the Pacific, the military top brass did a complete about-face. Mrs. R. was terrific. She never complained. She never demanded any exceptional services. She wore her uniform proudly, ate what they gave her, slept where they put her, bathed in whatever facilities were available and was tireless in her activities. And if they issued an order, she obeyed.

Admiral William H. "Bull" Halsey, outspoken and irascible by nature, was a quick convert. In his memoirs, written a few years after the war, he wrote of the First Lady:

> *"Here is what [Eleanor Roosevelt] did in twelve hours: she inspected two Navy hospitals, took a boat to an officer's rest home and had lunch there, returned and inspected an Army hospital, reviewed the 2nd Marine Raider Battalion (her son Jimmy had been its executive officer), made*

a speech at a service club, attended a reception, and was guest of honor at a dinner given by General Harmon.

When I say that she inspected those hospitals, I don't mean that she shook hands with the chief medical officer, glanced into a sunroom and left. I mean that she went into every ward, stopped at every bed, and spoke to every patient: What was his name? How did he feel? Was there anything he needed? Could she take a message home for him? I marveled at her hardihood, both physical and mental. She walked for miles, and she saw patients who were grievously and gruesomely wounded. But I marveled most at their expressions as she leaned over them. It was a sight I will never forget."

She not only visited every ward in the hospitals and infirmaries, she visited the military bases and ships. She kept a detailed notebook of names and families, dates and places, and diligently wrote personally to all their mothers and wives and sweethearts. All were heroes in her letters, which she knew would be saved and treasured for posterity. And she dutifully attended to the high-level politics of war, appearing at the obligatory luncheons and dinners. The men loved her. So did the brass, and they were not a bunch easily swayed.

The Uniform Roundup

Many First Ladies and First Ladies-to-be have visited the troops in wartime situations. Martha Washington was *with her husband* at Valley Forge, and Morristown and wherever he wanted her to go.

Margaret Taylor, a professional army wife for four decades, always traveled *with her husband* whenever it was safe. She was complimented by her husband (and later President) General Zachary Taylor, saying "she was just as much a soldier as I was."

Julia Grant encamped *with her husband* through much of the

Civil War. Lucy Hayes visited her husband's camps frequently, tending to him personally when he was wounded.

Mary Lincoln periodically went *with her husband* to review the troops during the Civil War. She also visited the wounded at the makeshift hospitals in Washington, usually going alone, and with no fanfare.

Visiting veterans' hospitals has always been an accepted activity for every sitting First Lady, and even today, whoever she is, she makes rounds periodically.

But other than in perhaps "honorary" uniforms for photo-op sessions, no other sitting First Lady besides Eleanor Roosevelt has worn a uniform specifically to travel with the military in an overseas war zone in the midst of a world war. And she went *without her husband.*

Even those battle-hardened generals who were not fond of their Commander-in-Chief tipped their hats to his lady.

$\mathcal{M}$rs. $\mathcal{R}$'s $\mathcal{V}$alise

There is an iconic photograph of Eleanor Roosevelt, taken later in her life, looking her usual frumpy self. Actually, there are a few similar photos, but in this one, she is dressed in a nondescript baggy suit, sensible shoes, a hat of no importance, and a sorry-looking but fashionable-for-the-time foxtail neck-wrap. In her right hand is an ordinary handbag and two briefcases. In her left hand, a valise, packed with the usual nightwear and change of clothing. It is Eleanor, pure and simple.

Most historians consider Eleanor Roosevelt to be the first *modern* First Lady—a woman with her own interests, agendas, purpose and accomplishments. First Ladies today, of course, are expected to have their own agendas, interests and purpose—along with substantive accomplishments. They are also expected to manage the White House social obligations, oversee its maintenance and decor, supervise traditional events, make dozens of appearances and speeches each week, pose for photographs, be interviewed by journalists, and still be attractive, well-dressed and groomed, and maintain unflagging energy and a pleasant disposition. *For free.*

They also have a large government-paid staff to help them in those duties.

The Eleanor Difference

By the time Mrs. Roosevelt became First Lady in 1933, she was nearly fifty and had a solid resume of visible and personal political activity behind her. Her husband Franklin, crippled by polio in 1921, had risen to the country's highest office despite his infirmities. It is said that Eleanor was initially unhappy about her forthcoming role. She did not want to be locked into the traditional First Lady tea-pouring image of her predecessors, nor did she want to relinquish any of the social and political activities that had become an important part of her life.

FDR assured her that she would not be required to give up anything, nor spend too much time on the mundane aspects of First Ladyhood. He needed her to be his eyes and ears, since his ability to get around was so limited. It was a task she had done for a decade.

Mrs. Roosevelt had no staff, only a secretary. Since she was generally indifferent to the day-to-day maintenance of the White House, she gratefully assigned those functions to either the White House housekeeper, or to FDR's secretary. So with little personal help other than Malvina "Tommy" Thompson, Eleanor Roosevelt developed her own agenda. She wrote a daily syndicated newspaper column; she chaired dozens of meetings for dozens of organizations, both at the White House and at remote locations; she championed scores of social causes; she developed her own friendships and political allies; and she still made the obligatory appearance at all the White House events where a First Lady presence is expected. And she never forgot a family birthday or anniversary and seemed to have time for everything.

On the Road

Eleanor Roosevelt's travel schedule was extensive and exhausting. She rarely turned down an invitation to speak for some worthy issue that she espoused. During the 1920s she drove her own car, but as First Lady she had a driver for local distances. Mostly she took trains and planes, without a Secret Service detail or an advance team. She either went alone or with Tommy. There was no fanfare and no crowds at the station, going or coming.

Even after twelve years as First Lady, Eleanor Roosevelt continued her non-stop travels practically until she died at age seventy-eight. It included many years as a United Nations delegate, teaching classes at Hunter College, and her endless lists of worthwhile enterprises to which she generously lent her name, prestige, time, and frequently, donated her own private funds.

She still required no formal escort other than a secretary, and, occasionally, as she got older, a grandson. When she was asked what she believed to be the most important attribute a First Lady must have, she was characteristic in her avoidance of the usual platitudes. "Good health," she said. And she meant it.

One needs to remember that Mrs. Roosevelt was not merely a Roosevelt by marriage. She was also a Roosevelt by birth. Her father's brother was Theodore Roosevelt, the man of boundless energy and interests. That energy was in her blood.

Thus the well-known photograph. She always carried her own valise.

$\mathcal{E}$LIZABETH (Bess) $\mathcal{V}$IRGINIA $\mathcal{W}$ALLACE $\mathcal{T}$RUMAN

Born: February 13, 1885

Place of Birth: Independence, MO

Parents: David Willock Wallace; Margaret Gates Wallace

Marriage: June 28, 1919

Children: Mary Margaret Truman Daniel

First Lady: 1945-1953

Date of Death: October 18, 1982

Place of Burial: Truman Library, Independence, MO

$\mathcal{B}$otanical $\mathcal{G}$arden of $\mathcal{H}$ats

$\mathcal{T}$o twentieth- and twenty-first-century scholars as well as general observers, the two First Ladies who followed Eleanor Roosevelt are usually considered disappointing. They did not do very much, but nobody seemed to mind. How come? Elizabeth "Bess" Wallace Truman is known mostly for her obvious dislike of the fishbowl life of First Ladydom. During the nearly eight years as the nation's Chief Occupantess, she was memorable for only two things: christening an aircraft with little success, and her view of the main duty of the President's Wife.

A photograph of Bess Wallace Truman, in a somber black suit and black hat, taken as her husband was hurriedly sworn in, shows a woman decidedly uncomfortable with the profound change that had just occurred. Franklin D. Roosevelt had died; Harry S. Truman, Vice President for less than three months, was now the nation's chief executive. If one looks at her photograph closely, one might even detect some anger: her life was changing profoundly as well, something she did not suffer gladly.

Her immediate predecessor, Eleanor Roosevelt, was a politically active woman in her own right, who gave her own weekly press conferences in addition to her numerous other activities. Mrs. Roosevelt, perhaps expecting that her precedent would be continued, generously offered to accompany Mrs. Truman to her first press conference with Washington's women journalists, and guide her over the shoals, as it were.

Mrs. Truman was uneasy and disinclined. She requested all questions to be submitted in writing. The ladies of the press obliged with a long list. Only one question was answered: *June 28, 1919*, her wedding date. Everything else was marked *no comment*, a Missouri mule euphemism for *none of your business*. Bess Truman was from Independence, Missouri, a town name befitting her. Her first press conference was also her last.

The Reasons for the Reluctance

Some people are not outgoing by nature. Some zealously guard their privacy. Bess Wallace was sociable enough. She had a bunch of old school chums that were friends for life, and hers was a very long one at nearly one hundred years. As Mrs. Senator Truman, she made pleasant friendships among Congressional wives, especially once they discovered she was a crackerjack bridge player.

Mostly, though, Bess was a homebody, devoted to her husband, their daughter Margaret, and her mother. Madge Wallace was a peculiar woman, difficult on her best day, which had long past.

Bess had a great secret to protect. When she was eighteen, her alcoholic father stood in their bathtub and put a bullet in his brain. In 1903, suicide was a huge scandal. The eccentric Mrs. Wallace became even more difficult and Bess indisputably had to manage the household and family, which included her three younger brothers. Any personal dreams she had for an education or career were immediately dropped. She was needed at home.

Even though her father's suicide was decades old and any scandal was likely forgotten by 1945, when Truman became President, Bess' newfound prominence as First Lady left her vulnerable to having her past unearthed, her privacy invaded, or worse—having her now-elderly and difficult mother upset all over again.

The Hat(s) Story

One of the only quotes attributed to the generally unquotable First Lady Truman was in answer to what *she* thought was the most important task of her office. Bess replied tersely, "To sit beside her husband, keep still, and make sure her hat is on straight." She usually checked the mirror, and her hat was always straight, but mostly at a formidable, if not pugnacious, angle.

Hats of course, come in all colors, styles, trims and the stuff that fashion dictates from season to season. Thus most women had dozens of hats: spring, summer, fall and winter, formal and casual. Bess probably had a closet full of them—enough to rate an interesting exhibit of its own at the Truman Library. Like Bess Truman herself, the hats are generally nondescript, and certainly not style-setting or remarkable except for a couple of oddball chapeaux—one was a triangular shaped concoction with tassels, looking part Mexican sombrero and part Bozo the Clown. It must be seen to be believed. Another conception from her youth was a flat boater type, bedecked with ribbons, and only needing a dangling price tag to rival the Grand Ol' Opry star, Minnie Pearl.

The rest of the hats in the exhibit are exactly what one would expect from a woman whose First Lady uniform consisted mainly of boxy, man-tailored suits in either black, navy or various shades of gray, and a white or pastel-colored blouse. The hats were made of felt or straw or taffeta or other popular hat fabrics. There were feathers, fruit, beads, and an occasional bird or ribbon. Sometimes a veil.

But mostly, the hats were floral. Name a color, Bess had a hat with said color flowers in every shade. Name a kind of flower, and Bess had a conservatory of every description. Rosebuds and geraniums, daisies, lilies, petunias, pansies and assorted other posies. They were accentuated with leaves, ferns and foliage.

Harry Truman, in response to an unflattering remark about his sixty-year-old wife's beauty, commented sharply, "She looks exactly like what a woman her age ought to look like." He had zero tolerance for swipes at his women-folk. But he was probably right about Bess' looks. She really *was* like what a woman her age ought to look like in the 1940s. And her hats were exactly like what a Bess Truman hat ought to look like.

And she did as she proclaimed. She kept silent and made sure whatever hat she wore was on straight.

The Airplane Story

But Bess Truman, with or without a hat, also had a good sense of humor. At least, so said her family.

By the 1940s, First Ladies were readily dispatched on their own to perform moderate ceremonial appearances: groundbreaking, ribbon cutting, wreath laying and flower accepting. Bess always did whatever duties her husband requested. Nothing less, but seldom anything more.

When a new aircraft was about to be launched, Mrs. T. and her daughter Margaret were guests of honor at the anointment. She was dressed in her trademark shapeless suit, this time with a floral corsage, and a black bonnet with a ribbon and white trim decorating the brim. She swung a seemingly unbreakable bottle of champagne at the side of the plane. Time and again the First Lady took a full cut at that plane with a bottle that refused to yield. It had not been pre-scored to weaken the side. Bess, who had been notably athletic in her youth, was embarrassed and angry, all the more because the newsreel cameras were rolling for public consumption, and certain to be shown in every movie theatre in the country.

She was furious when she returned to the White House and bitterly complained to her equally incensed husband, who did not want the First Lady of the Land, *his wife,* humiliated. He immediately demanded the one and only copy of the newsreel footage.

The three Trumans—Harry, Bess and Margaret—viewed the film privately, and they howled! Margaret later wrote that she was rolling on the floor, and her father had tears running down his face. It was not an embarrassment. It was a hilarious *Lucy* moment. Nobody was laughing at Bess Truman, First Lady. They were laughing at a very *very* funny situation. People still laugh when the clip is shown. It is still funny.

Other First Ladies have done worse than provide a good laugh for the American people. And Bess did it silently, and her hat was on straight. And if she thought it was funny, she kept it *under* her hat.

$\mathcal{M}$AMIE $\mathcal{G}$ENEVA $\mathcal{D}$OUD $\mathcal{E}$ISENHOWER

Born: November 14, 1896

Place of Birth: Boone, Iowa

Parents: John Sheldon Doud; Elivera Carlson Doud

Marriage: July 1, 1916

Children: David Doud Eisenhower (d. age 3); John Sheldon Doud
Eisenhower

First Lady: 1953-1961

Date of Death: November 1, 1979

Place of Burial: Eisenhower Library, Abilene, KS

A *Pink Bed Jacket*—
and *Other Pink Stuff*

*M*ost women under fifty have no clue what a *bed jacket* is. It is more or less an archaic item. But fifty or sixty years ago, most ladies of a certain age and social status had a bed jacket in their lingerie drawer. It was, as one might presume, a garment to be worn in bed over a nightie. It could be worn to ward off a chill in an already indisposed woman, or as a slight affectation for a pampered breakfast in bed. Mamie Eisenhower used it both ways.

Pampered Little Rich Girl

Mamie Geneva Doud Eisenhower, Iowa-born, Colorado bred, came from a very well-to-do family. The Douds lived in Denver's most fashionable section, where their daughter was appropriately pampered and petted.

Mamie had suffered a touch of rheumatic fever in her youth, and her health would be considered somewhat delicate thereafter. According to those who knew her well, she was very much inclined to take to her bed at the slightest hint of ailment. Thus her bed jackets.

The Douds were wealthy enough to take winter vacations, and on one such trip to San Antonio, Texas, she met her destiny in the person of Second Lt. Dwight D. Eisenhower, recently graduated from West Point. He thought she was the cutest thing he had ever seen.

Ike and Mamie were married when she was only nineteen, and while the Douds adored Ike, and considered him their son as long as they lived, they were genuinely concerned about their daughter's much-too-young marriage. Could a rather spoiled teenager make a go of being an army wife?

The Talents of Mamie

Mamie Eisenhower was not a scholarly woman. Her education was average, her abilities, a ladylike *C*. Nor was Mamie a domestic woman. Even though she would come to look like everybody's cookie-baking grandma, her cooking skills were limited. She once said that she tossed the salad while Ike grilled the steaks. Her sewing skills did not exist. Nor did junior officer quarters on army bases take long to keep tidy. She had no strong interests or hobbies to occupy her time.

But Mamie had some hidden talents that would stand her in excellent stead in years to come.

First, she had a wall-to-wall smile, very much like her husband. Her face lit up. It was appealing. Just like Ike's.

Secondly, she was very social and made friends easily. Just like Ike. Throughout their lives, and throughout literally dozens of moves, their house, wherever it was, became *Club Eisenhower,* open for cocktail parties, card games and potluck dinners. Everybody came, and most of their friends became so for life.

Mamie Becomes a Celebrity

For nearly twenty-five years, Mamie Eisenhower was happy to be wife to a mid-level Army officer. It was the Depression. No one was leaving a steady job and the reliable income of military life, so promotions were limited. There was no upward availability. Ike believed he would retire no higher than Colonel.

World War II changed all that when Colonel Eisenhower was promoted over more than a hundred officers with more seniority. By the end of the war, Ike had five stars on his shoulder, and was *the* General with tickertape parades in his honor. After five years of wartime separation along with constant worry, Mamie was not about the leave *her* General's side. She was going where he was going. Period. And they went everywhere.

By 1952, the sixty-one-year-old general finally succumbed to the lure of politics and agreed to be the Republican presidential candidate. The result was a foregone conclusion. Everybody liked Ike.

Mamie, at fifty-five, was a breath of fresh air to the new postwar generation. She was cute. She was feminine. She wore pink because it was her favorite color. Pink dresses, hats, purses, gloves, and, according to those who knew, pink undies and nighties. She still had a waistline. Her shoes were not in the sensible category. They were high heels—in pink! Her *Mamie bangs* became an instant hit with the public. *Cute* was definitely in.

For twenty years, the American First Lady had been either the formal Lou Hoover, the homely, independent and highly visible Eleanor Roosevelt, or the quasi-unfriendly Bess Truman. While they all had their virtues and accomplishments, no one would call any of them attractive, or fashionable or exuding feminine charm. For certain, they were not *cute.*

Mamie the Campaigner

Mamie was definitely hot copy. The stylish princess-line dresses of the early 1950s looked good on her. Her high heels came in fashionable shapes and colors. She wore makeup. And the American public—men *and* women—took to her as much as they took to Ike.

Mamie surprised everyone, including herself. She positively enjoyed the campaign trail, a political obligation that her predecessors, including Eleanor Roosevelt, did not care for. She was happy to pose for the cameras; to accept bouquets; to throw kisses to schoolchildren; to wave and grin along with Ike. His political aides, who had been prepared to shoo her away, were not only pleasantly surprised, they were delighted at what an asset Mrs. Ike was to the campaign. The public adored her. Even better, she did not get in the way. If she had opinions, she kept them to herself. She could be trusted in public.

Of course they won the election. They were unbeatable.

A New-ish First Lady?

The changing and challenging role of the First Lady pioneered by the energetic and independent Eleanor Roosevelt did not set an immediate precedent. It took nearly two decades before it settled into its present status and expectations. Mamie Eisenhower was a First Lady in transition.

She had no intention of pursuing an agenda of her own. She had no desire to interfere in politics. She had no particular interests other than being first and foremost *Mrs. Ike,* the General's wife. She would, of course, undertake whatever tasks the President asked of her, as did Bess Truman, and she would grace their social obligations with natural charm, but she was neither inclined nor interested in pursuing anything other than the traditional and socially acceptable First Lady duties. If she had any outside interest, it was decorating the Eisenhower's new home in Gettysburg, Pennsylvania. It was the first and only house the Eisenhowers ever owned, and Mamie had waited for it for nearly forty years.

Social obligations had always been a necessary part of being a military officer's wife, and Mrs. Ike was equal to the task, in and out of the White House, or at their Gettysburg farm, where they loved to bring personal friends and important visitors. Those obligations had soared to the highest level when Ike was a five-star general. Mamie planned and hosted not only with the ease of her personality, but also with the assurance of a general's wife, just like Martha Washington and Julia Grant. In the White House, entertaining guests was no different, but perhaps for the first time in history, the head-of-state visitors who came in droves were mostly old friends they had known for years. When Ike became President, he was arguably the best-known person in the world.

The First Lady in Transition

As First Lady, Mamie treated herself to a leisurely start: breakfast in bed, wearing one of her pink bed jackets, and often with a pink ribbon tied little-girl style around her short Mamie-banged bobbed haircut. Her secretary or the head housekeeper would join her in the bedroom for coffee and work: planning the day. But if the FLOTUS was feeling just a tad iffy, that bed jacket stayed on, and Mamie stayed in bed.

The journalists may have lost interest in Bess Truman, but their interest was revved up to high gear with the new First Lady. Mamie was wonderful copy, not so much for anything she did or said, but for just being herself. She liked pink and the reporters reported it and pink became the color of the 1950s. Short little Mamie-bangs were seen on women everywhere, made doubly popular by an adorable young movie star, Audrey Hepburn. And when Mamie wore a dress credited to a particular designer, which she often did, it was immediately copied and promoted, and sold in stores from Bergdorf Goodman's to Macy's.

Whether or not she liked it or realized it, Mamie Eisenhower was a pivotal First Lady: the last one born in the nineteenth century, when women were only beginning to emerge from the protected cocoons. Mamie still loved living traditionally, which was under Ike's protective wing. But in her own way, she was also a new kind of First Lady—The First Lady as a celebrity just for being herself.

And pink stuff was definitely in. The usual pink accouterments: dresser sets and perfume bottles, towels, sheets and even typewriters. Then there was the fad of pink appliances in kitchens, including the stove and refrigerator. Pink fixtures in the bathroom, including tiles, tubs and even toilets and toilet seats. One story tells of Mamie moving into a hospital room next to where Ike was being watched carefully after one of his heart attacks. She demanded a new toilet seat—in pink. Standard pink toilet seats did not fit the standard hospital toilets. It was a nightmare trying to accommodate.

First Ladies who followed her would be firmly planted in the twentieth century. They would have twentieth-century notions of what a First Lady can accomplish on her own bully pulpit, and they would all use it for a variety of worthy enterprises. It is now expected.

Mamie Eisenhower has faded from interest over the years. Her performance as First Lady usually ranks no more than a ladylike C. And for whatever reasons, except for one famous hot pink suit, none of her successors have worn much pink.

$\mathcal{A}$cknowledgments

$\mathcal{W}$riting is always a solitary occupation. It is internal, but it is never completely "alone." Many others are involved to some degree. Some do not even know how much they contribute.

The First Ladies themselves have been my dear companions for two decades, and they never grow tiresome. There is always something to learn and appreciate.

My personal thanks go to the many docents, archivists and other staff members at various presidential sites, who have been generous with their time and assistance. In particular, I need to express sincere gratitude to Farron Smith at the Edith Bolling Wilson Birthplace Museum, who, over the years, has always been quick to respond to my questions and queries; to Michelle Guillon, Archives Director at the First Ladies' Historic Site, who promptly returned phone calls and was most helpful in providing some of the research and photos for the book; to Lynn Smith, Audio-Visual Archivist at the Herbert Hoover Presidential Library-Museum, who has a delightful sense of humor and who would be high on my list of "let's have coffee"; to Kerry Wood, Chief of Interpretation (Acting) at the William Howard Taft National Historic Site; to Sarah L. Malcolm, Archivist, Franklin

D. Roosevelt Presidential Library; to Pauline Pesterman at the Truman Library; and to staff members and volunteers at several other presidential sites who have been considerate and helpful. And of course, to the Library of Congress administrative staff for their help in navigating my way through their mazes of photographs.

Many thanks are also due to my various writers' groups in the Williamsburg, Virginia area. Our members are always generous with their comments, substantive recommendations, information, and above all, support.

To my "readers," Shelby Hawthorne, Louise Hamilton and Heather Voight, whose comments and suggestions were invaluable. To Narielle Living whose "u-turn" title suggestion I not only liked, but used.

To the staff of the Williamsburg Library, where I have become a fixture.

To my Lifelong Learning "students" at both the Christopher Wren Society (William & Mary) and Christopher Newport University who have encouraged and supported all my efforts, and who always ask the best questions.

To John Koehler and Joe Coccaro, my publisher and editor, for their confidence in me and their substantive help and guidance.

To my friends and family who are by now thoroughly tired of FLOTUS stories, but put up with me anyway.

And finally, to the memory of Laura G. Haywood, one of those rare strangers who show up in a life from time to time, and redirect everything.

Author's Notes

*A*ll the "stories" included in the book are based on true situations and true articles of clothing (unless indicated as metaphorical) albeit told as a "story" rather than as a factual document. A huge number of books and websites, articles and films have been utilized in preparing it. The "telling" of the stories, with whatever backgrounds and embellishments are needed to make it a story, is something else.

Stories have been neglected for generations for some unfathomable reason, especially since people have always loved a good story. They have flocked to movie and television versions of westerns and costume pieces, from Biblical epics to knights in armor to *Downton Abbey*. They love seeing the old clothing styles, the hats, the funny-looking shoes. They chuckle at the old-timey bathing "costumes" with pantaloons and stockings. They are incredulous that a gentleman was expected to put on his coat (i.e. suit jacket) just to answer his door. It boggles the mind that a swarthy, macho fellow could wear tights and short balloon pants and call himself a "conquistador." Hollywood may not be academic history, but if it is done well, it makes one enjoy the subject, and possibly want to delve a little further. I have tried to do similarly.

In my many talks, book signings, classes, etc., I am frequently asked why I choose to end my First Ladies with Mamie Eisenhower. After all, we have had ten more since then! This is a fair question, for which I have two answers.

First: Mamie Eisenhower is the last First Lady born in the nineteenth century. This is as good a place as any to put a period after the sentence. But it is also a simplistic answer.

The better answer is that somewhere around 1960, as an arbitrary date, all the rules changed for what is required (and now demanded) of a First Lady. Modern FLOTUSes are no longer simple and pleasant housewives, who, like Bess Truman, believed her main duty was "to keep her hat on straight." Today, they are all educated, and have likely had substantive careers prior to and even after marriage. They are required to do far more than accept bouquets, attend a grand opening of a school, answer their mail, suggest banquet napkin colors and occasionally supervise the daily maintenance of the White House, all of which they still do. But now they are also articulate public speakers, article writers, television and radio interviewees and fashion mavens. They are expected to be attractive, well-groomed, and even under the most trying circumstances, to maintain a pleasant disposition. How can they possibly compare to the earlier mistresses of the White House?

Early First Ladies had little in the way of "staff." The White House, of course, had sufficient servants, so a First Lady never had to handle laundry (other than Abigail Adams) or iron a gown or wash a dish. But with the possible exception of a personal ladies' maid, there was no assistance other than a niece or daughter to help with part-time hosting or letter writing. That changed around the beginning of the twentieth century when a social secretary was becoming a necessity. It would not be until the mid-twentieth century that a First Lady "staff" would be required.

Even the peripatetic and seemingly inexhaustible Eleanor Roosevelt, a First Lady decades ahead of her time, managed with only a personal secretary. Then again, Mrs. R. was never overly concerned with housekeeping or fashion.

Part of that "staff" today is used exclusively to manage the First Lady's wardrobe, which is extensive. Between near constant travel, perhaps four or five personal appearances a day, speeches, meetings, interviews, photo-ops, meet-and-greets, breakfasts, luncheons, teas and dinners, banquets, balls, and maybe a little down-time, a First Lady may reasonably be expected to change her clothing four or five times a day.

Today's First Lady is dressed and gowned and even sweatsuited by world-famous designers who vie constantly for her favor. Detailed records are kept of what the First Lady wears every day, occasion by occasion, to ensure that her outfits are not seen twice before the same "audience." Once she removes an item, it is whisked away to be cleaned or laundered—or perhaps given a once-over with the iron.

There is no comparison. Certainly not a fair comparison. So the decision to end with Mamie becomes a personal one, so that the "old gals" are not completely overshadowed by the modern ones. They are far too wonderful to be summarily dismissed. They are our "national great-grandmas". They are the ones who need me.

And finally, my purpose has always been to make history as enjoyable to the reader as it has been to me.

$\mathcal{B}$ibliography

To spare the reader from the distractions of footnotes, direct quotations have been avoided as much as possible. Nevertheless, dozens of sources have been used in preparing this book.

To make the bibliography less repetitious, it has been subdivided according to general First Lady additional reference material (such as general presidential, White House, elections, etc.), online reference sources and, finally, specific First Lady references.

It is also been the author's personal delight to have visited most presidential sites, and to have learned so much from their docents and staff members. Web addresses are included.

I have not included Wikipedia, although it was used as a reference for convenient basic information.

General Books and Reference Sources:

Adler, Bill (with Norman King)—*All in the First Family: The President's Kinfolk*—G.P. Putnam's Sons, 1982

Anderson, Alice E. and Baxendale, Hadley V.—*Behind Every Successful President*—Spi Books, 1992

Anthony, Carl—*First Ladies: The Saga of the Presidents' Wives and their Power 1789-1961*—William Morrow, 1990

Barzman, Sol—*The First Ladies*—Cowles Book Company, 1970

Boller, Paul—*Presidential Wives: An Anecdotal History*—Oxford University Press, 1988

Caroli, Betty Boyd—*Inside the White House: First Ladies from Martha Washington to Hillary Clinton*—Canopy, 1992

—*First Ladies: From Martha Washington to Hillary Clinton*—Doubleday Direct, 1997

Foster, Feather Schwartz—*The First Ladies From Martha Washington to Mamie Eisenhower: An Intimate Portrait of the Women Who Shaped America*—Sourcebooks, 2011

Furman, Bess—*White House Profile*—The Bobbs-Merrill Company, 1951

Garrison, Webb—*White House Ladies: Fascinating Tales and Colorful Curiosities*—Rutledge Hill Press, 1996

Gould, Lewis L.—*American First Ladies: Their Lives and Their Legacy*—Routledge, 2014

Graddy, Lisa Kathleen & Pastan, Amy—*The Smithsonian First Ladies Collection*—Smithsonian Books, 2014

Healy, Diana Dixon—*America's First Ladies: Private Lives of the Presidential Wives*—Atheneum, 1988

Hoover, Irwin (Ike)—*42 Years in the White House*—Houghton Mifflin, 1934

Jeffries, Ona Griffin—*In and Out of the White House* - Wilfred Funk, Inc. 1960

Kelly, C. Brian—*Best Little Stories from the White House*—Cumberland House, 2003

Logan, Mrs. John L.—*Thirty Years in Washington, Or, Life and Scenes in Our Nation's Capital*—1901

Means, Marianne—*The Woman in the White House*—The New American Library 1963

Melick, Arden Davis—*Wives of the Presidents*—Hammond, Inc. 1972

Schneider, Dorothy and Schneider, Carl J.—*First Ladies: A Biographical Dictionary*—Facts on File, 2010

Seale, William—*The President's House: A History*—White House Historical Assn., 1986

Swain, Susan—*First Ladies: Presidential Historians on the Lives of 45 Iconic Women*—Public Affairs, 2015

Thomas, E.H. Gwynne—*The Presidential Families: From George Washington to Ronald Reagan*—Hippocrene Books, 1989

Truman, Margaret—*First Ladies: An Intimate Group Portrait of White House Wives*—Ballantine Books, 1997

—*The President's House: 1800 to the Present: A First Daughter Shares the History and Secrets of the World's Most Famous Home*—Ballantine Books, 2003

Wead, Doug—*All the Presidents' Children*—Atria Books, 2003

West, J.B. (with Mary Lynn Kotz)—*Upstairs at the White House: My Life with the First Ladies*—Coward, McCann & Geoghegen, 1973

C-SPAN.org broadcasts on both the presidents and the first ladies.

General Website Reference Sources

Below are listed online sources, each having numerous sections, providing invaluable general information.

www.firstladies.org

www.whitehouse.gov

www.carlanthonyonlie.com

www.abrahamlincolnonline.org

www.c-span.org/first ladies

www.firstladiesof america.com

www.biography.com

www.millercenter.org

www.history.com

Martha Washington:

Bourne, Miriam Anne—*First Family: George Washington and his Intimate Relations*—W.W. Norton & Co., 1982

Brady, Patricia—*Martha Washington: An American Life*—Penguin Books, 2006

Bryan, Helen—*Martha Washington: First Lady of Liberty*—John Wiley, 2002

Chadwick, Bruce—*The General and Mrs. Washington*—Sourcebooks, 2005

Desmond, Alice Curtis—*Martha Washington, Our First Lady*—Dodd Mead, 1947

Niles, Blair—*Martha's Husband*—McGraw Hill, 1951

Randall, Willard Sterne—*George Washington: A Life*—Galahad Books, 2006

Thayne, Elswyth—*Mount Vernon Family*—Crowell-Collier, 1968

Wilson, Dorothy Clarke—*Lady Washington*—Doubleday, 1984

Presidential site, Mt. Vernon, VA: www.mountvernon.org
www.colonialmusic.org

Abigail Adams

Adams, James Truslow—*The Adams Family*—Blue Ribbon, 1932

Abigail Adams—*The Letters of John and Abigail Adams*—Penguin Classics, 2003

Barker-Benfield, G.J.—*Abigail and John Adams: The Americanization of Sensibility*—University of Chicago Press, 2010

Bober, Natalie S.—*Abigail Adams: Witness to a Revolution*—Atheneum, 1995

Ellis, Joseph (foreword)—*My Dearest Friend*—Belknap Press, 2010
    – *First Family: Abigail and John Adams*—Alfred A.Knopf, 2010

Gelles, Edith—*Abigail and John: Portrait of a Marriage*—William Morrow, 2009

Holton, Woody—*Abigail Adams*—The Free Press, 2009

Jacobs, Diane—*Dear Abigail: The Intimate Lives and Revolutionary Ideas of Abigail Adams and Her Two Remarkable Sisters*—Ballantine Books, 2014

Levin, Phyllis—*Abigail Adams*—St. Martin's Press—1987

McCullough, David—*John Adams*—Simon & Schuster, 2001

Nagel, Paul C.—*Descent from Glory: Four Generations of Adams Women*—Oxford University Press, 1983
    – *The Adams Women: Abigail and Louisa, Their Sisters and Daughters*—Harvard University Press, 1999

Russell, Francis—*ADAMS: An American Dynasty*—American Heritage, 1976

Shepherd, Jack—*The Adams Chronicles: Four Generations of Greatness*—Little Brown & Co., 1976

Whitney, Janet—*Abigail Adams*—Atlantic, Little Brown, 1947

Withey, Lynne—*Dearest Friend: A Life of Abigail Adams*—The Free Press, 1981

Presidential site, Quincy, MA: www.nps.gov/adam

Dolley Madison

Allgor, Catherine—*Parlor Politics: In Which the Ladies of Washington Help Build a City and a Government*—University of Virginia Press, 2000

– *A Perfect Union: Dolley Madison and the Creation of the American Nation*—Henry Holt & Co., 2006

Anthony, Katharine—*Dolley Madison, Her Life and Times*—Doubleday & Co., 1949

Gerson, Noel B.—*The Velvet Glove*—Thomas Nelson, Inc., 1975

Howard, Hugh—*Mr. and Mrs. Madison's War: America's First Couple and the Second War of Independence*—Bloomsbury Press, 2012

Mattern, David B. and Shulman, Holly C. (eds)—*The Selected Letters of Dolley Payne Madison*—University of Virginia Press, 2003

Moore, Virginia—*The Madisons: A Biography*—McGraw Hill, 1976

Nolan, Jeanette Covert—*Dolley Madison*—Julian Messner, 1958

Presidential site, Orange County, VA: www.montpelier.org

Elizabeth Monroe

Allgor, Catherine—*Parlor Politics: In Which the Ladies of Washington Help Build a City and a Government*—University of Virginia Press, 2000

Unger, Harlow—*The Last Founding Father: James Monroe and a Nation's Call to Greatness*—DaCapo Press, 2010

Presidential site, Albemarle County, VA: www.ashlawnhighland.org

Presidential site, Fredericksburg, VA: www.jamesmonroemuseum.umw.edu/

Louisa Catherine Adams

Adams, Louisa Catherine and Hogan, Margaret A.—*A Traveled First Lady: Writings of Louisa Catherine Adams*—Belknap Press, 2014

Allgor, Catherine—*Parlor Politics: In Which the Ladies of Washington Help Build a City and a Government*—University of Virginia Press, 2000

Bobbe, Dorothie—*Mr. & Mrs. John Quincy Adams*—Minton Balch, 1950

Cook, Jane Hampton—*American Phoenix: John Quincy and Louisa Adams, The War of 1812, and the Exile that Saved American Independence*—Thomas Nelson, 2013

Nagel, Paul C.—*John Quincy Adams: A Public Life, A Private Life*—Knopf, 1997

  – *Descent from Glory: Four Generations of Adams Women*—Oxford University Press, 1983

  – *The Adams Women: Abigail and Louisa, Their Sisters and Daughters*—Harvard University Press, 1999

O'Brien, Michael—*Mrs. Adams in Winter: A Journey in the Last Days of Napoleon*—Farrar, Straus and Girous—2011

Shepherd, Jack—*The Adams Chronicles: Four Generations of Greatness*—Little Brown & Co. 1976

  – *Cannibals of the Heart: A Personal Biography of Louisa Catherine and John Quincy Adams*—McGraw Hill, 1980

Unger, Harlow—*John Quincy Adams*—DaCapo Press, 2012

Presidential site, Quincy, MA: www.nps.gov/adam/

Rachel Donelson Jackson

Brands, H.W.—*Andrew Jackson: His Life and Times*—Doubleday, 2005

Burstein, Andrew—*The Passions of Andrew Jackson*—Borzoi/Knopf, 2003

Byrd, Max—*Jackson: A Novel*—Bantam, 1997

Marszalek, John F.—*The Petticoat Affair*—Free Press, 1997

Meacham, Jon—*American Lion: Andrew Jackson in the White House*—Random House, 2008

Remini, Robert—*The Life of Andrew Jackson*—Harper & Row, 1988

Presidential site, Nashville, TN: www.thehermitage.com

Julia Gardiner Tyler

Craypol, Edward P.—*John Tyler, the Accidental President*—University of North Carolina Press, 2006

Seager, Robert, II—*And Tyler Too: A Biography of John and Julia Gardiner Tyler*—Historic Sherwood Forest Corporation, 2003

Presidential site, Charles City, VA: www.sherwoodforest.org

Sarah Childress Polk

Anson, Fanny and Nelson—*Memorials of Sarah Childress Polk, wife of the 11th President of the United States*—Reprint Company, 1974

Dusinberre, William—*Slavemaster President*—Oxford University Press, 2003

Peterson, Barbara Bennett—*Sarah Childress Polk*—Nova History Publications, 2002

Presidential site, Columbia, TN: www.jameskpolk.com

Jane Appleton Pierce

Covell, Ann—*Jane Means Appleton Pierce: US First Lady (1853-1857): Her Family, Life and Times* –Hamilton Books, 2013

Shenkman, Richard—*Presidential Ambition: Gaining Power at Any Cost*—Harper, 1999

Presidential site, Concord, NH www.piercemanse.org

Harriet Lane

Stern, Milton—*America's Bachelor President and the First Lady*—PublishAmerica, 2004

Presidential site: Lancaster, PA: http://www.nps.gov/nr/travel/presidents/james_buchanan_wheatland.html

Mary Todd Lincoln

Baker, Jean Harvey—*Mary Todd Lincoln: A Biography*—W.W. Norton, 1987

Baynes, Julia Taft—*Tad Lincoln's Father*—Little, Brown, 1931

Berry, Stephen—*House of Abraham*—Houghton Mifflin Harcourt, 2007

Clinton, Catherine—*Mrs. Lincoln: A Life*—Harper, 2009

Colver, Anne—*Mr. Lincoln's Wife*—Holt, Rinehart, 1965

Epstein, Daniel Mark—*The Lincolns, Portrait of a Marriage*—Ballantine Books, 2008

Hambly, Barbara—*The Emancipator's Wife*—Bantam Books, 2005

Helm, Katherine—*Mary, Wife of Lincoln*—Harper & Bros. 1928

Keckley, Elizabeth—*Behind the Scenes, or Thirty Years a Slave, And Four Years in the White House*—Cosimo Classics, 2009

Lachman, Charles—*The Last Lincolns*—Union Square Press, 2008

Randall, Ruth Painter—*Mary Lincoln: Biography of a Marriage*—Little Brown, 1953

Ross, Ishbel—*The President's Wife: Mary Todd Lincoln*—G.P. Putnam's Sons, 1973

Schreiner, Samuel A.—*The Trials of Mrs. Lincoln*—Donald I. Fine, 1987

Turner, Justin G. and Turner, Linda Levitt (eds.)—*Mary Todd Lincoln: Her Life and Letters*—Knopf, New York, 1972

Van der Heuvel, Gerry—*Crowns of Thorns and Glory*—E.P. Dutton, 1988

Winkler, H. Donald—*The Women in Lincoln's Life*—Rutledge Hill, 2001

www.internetstones.com

www.abrahamlincolnonline.org

Presidential site: Springfield, IL: www.nps.gov/liho

First Ladies site: Lexington, KY: www.mlthouse.org

Julia Dent Grant

Flood, Charles B.—*Grant's Final Victory*—DaCapo Press, 2011

Grant, Julia Dent—*The Personal Memoirs of Julia Grant (Mrs. Ulysses S. Grant)*—G.P. Putnam's Sons, 1975

Grant, U.S.—*Memoirs and Selected Letters (1839-1865)*—Library of America, 1990

Korda, Michael—*Ulysses S. Grant: The Unlikely Hero*—Harper, 2013

Lewis, Lloyd—*Captain Sam Grant*—Little Brown, 1950

McFeeley, Wm. S.—*Grant: A Biography*—W.W. Norton, 1981

Ross, Ishbel—*The General's Wife: The Life of Mrs. Ulysses S. Grant*—Dodd Mead & Co., 1959

Todd, Helen—*A Man Named Grant*—Houghton Mifflin, 1940

Presidential site: St. Louis, MO: http://www.nps.gov/ulsg/learn/historyculture/jdgrant.htm

Lucy Webb Hayes

Geer, Emily Apt—*First Lady: The Life of Lucy Webb Hayes*—Kent State University Press, 1984

Williams, Harry T. (ed).—*Hayes: The Diary of a President*—David McKay, 1964

http://whitemountainart.com/about-3/artists/daniel-huntington-1816-1906-2/

Presidential site: Fremont, OH: www.rbhayes.org

Frances Folsom Cleveland

Brodsky, Alyn—*Grover Cleveland: A Study in Character*—St. Martin's Press, 2000

Carpenter, Frank G.—*"Carp's Washington"*—McGraw Hill, 1960

Cross, Wilbur and Novotny, Ann—*White House Weddings*—David McKay Co., 1967

Dunlap, Annette—*FRANK: The Story of Frances Folsom Cleveland, America's Youngest First Lady* –Excelsior Editions, 2009

Jeffers, H. Paul—*An Honest President*—William Morrow, 2000

Jeffries, Ona Griffin—*In and Out of the White House*—Wilfred Funk, Inc. 1960

Logan, Mrs. John L.—*Thirty Years in Washington, Or, Life and Scenes in Our Nation's Capital*—1901

Caroline Scott Harrison

Carpenter, Frank G.—*"Carp's Washington"*—McGraw Hill, 1960

Jeffries, Ona Griffin—*In and Out of the White House*—Wilfred Funk, Inc. 1960

Seale, Williams—*The President's House*—The White House Historical Association, 2008

Sievers, Harry—*Benjamin Harrison: Hoosier Statesman*—University Publishers, 1959

Presidential site: Indianapolis, IN: www.presidentbenjaminharrison.org

Ida Saxton McKinley

Leech, Margaret—*In the Days of McKinley*—Harper & Bros. 1959

Morgan, H. Wayne—*William McKinley and His America*—Kent State University Press, 2004

Schneider, Dorothy and Schneider, Carl J.—*First Ladies: A Biographical Dictionary*—Facts on File, 2001

Traxel, David—*1898: The Tumultuous Year of Victory, Invention, Internal Strife and Industrial Expansion that saw the Birth of the American Century*—Alfred A. Knopf, 1998

Edith Carow Roosevelt

Brands, H.S.—*TR: The Last Romantic*—Basic Books, 1997

Caroli, Betty Boyd—*The Roosevelt Women: A Portrait in Five Generations*—Basic Books, 1998

Cordery, Stacy—*Alice: Alice Roosevelt Longworth, from White House Princess to Washington Power Broker*—Viking, 2007

Dalton, Kathleen—*A Strenuous Life*—Vintage, 2004

Donald, Aida—*Lion in the White House*—Basic Books, 2007

Hagedorn, Hermann—*The Roosevelt Family of Sagamore Hill*—Macmillan, 1954

Morris, Sylvia Jukes—*Edith Kermit Roosevelt*—Modern Library, 2001

Wilson, Dorothy Clarke—*Alice and Edith: A Biographical Novel of the Wives of Theodore Roosevelt*—Doubleday, 1989

Presidential site: Oyster Bay, NY: http://www.nps.gov/nr/travel/presidents/t_roosevelt_sagamore_hill.html

Helen Herron Taft

Anthony, Carl Sferrazza—*Nellie Taft: The Unconventional First Lady of the Ragtime Era*—Harper Collins, 2009

Butt, Archie—*The Intimate Letters of Archie Butt, Military Aide*—Doubleday & Company, 1930

Ross, Ishbel—*An American Family: The Tafts, 1678-1964*—World Publishing Co., 1964

Taft, Mrs. William Howard—*Recollections of Full Years*—Dodd, Mead, 1914

www.etiquetteer,cin/category/nellie-taft

www.stretching-it.com/stret/taft/Taft_humor_pg3.htm

Presidential site: Cincinnati, OH: http://www.nps.gov/wiho/index.htm

Ellen Axson Wilson

Axson, Stockton—*Brother Woodrow: A Memoir of Woodrow by Stockton Axson*—Princeton University Press, 1993

McAdoo, Eleanor Wilson—*The Woodrow Wilson*—Curtis Publishing, 1936

—*The Priceless Gift: The Love Letters of Woodrow Wilson and Ellen Axson Wilson* —McGraw Hill, 1962

Miller, Kristie—*Ellen and Edith: Woodrow Wilson's First Ladies*— University Press of Kansas, 2010

Saunders, Frances—*Ellen Axson Wilson: First Lady Between Two Worlds*—University of North Carolina Press, 1985

Presidential site: Staunton, VA http://www.woodrowwilson.org/museum/the-birthplace-the-manse

Edith Bolling Galt Wilson

Hatch, Alden—*Edith Bolling Wilson: First Lady Extraordinary*— Dodd, Mead, 1961

Levin, Phyllis—*Edith and Woodrow: The Wilson White House*—Lisa Drew Books, Scribner, 2001

Miller, Kristie—*Ellen and Edith: Woodrow Wilson's First Ladies*— University Press of Kansas, 2010

Ross, Ishbel—*Power With Grace: The Life Story of Mrs. Woodrow Wilson*—Putnam, 1975

Shachtman, Tom—*Edith and Woodrow: A Presidential Romance*— Putnam Publishing Group, 1981

Smith, Gene—*When the Cheering Stopped*—William Morrow, 1964

Tribble, Edwin (ed.)—*President in Love: The Courtship Letters of Woodrow Wilson and Edith Bolling Galt*—Houghton Mifflin, 1981

Wilson, Edith Bolling—*My Memoir*—Bobbs Merrill, 1939

Presidential site: Washington, DC: www.woodrowwilsonhouse.org

First Lady site: Wytheville, VA: http://edithbollingwilson.org/

www.smithsonianmag.com/history/a-symbol-that-failed-149514383/

Florence Kling Harding

Anthony, Carl Sferrazza—*Florence Harding: The First Lady, The Jazz Age, and the Death of America's Most Scandalous President*—Harper Perennial, 1999

Mee, Charles L. Jr.—*The Ohio Gang: The World of Warren G. Harding: An Historical Entertainment* –Henry Holt & Co., 1983

Russell, Francis—*The Shadow of Blooming Grove: Warren G. Harding In His Times*—McGraw Hill 1968

Sinclair, Andrew—*The Available Man: Warren Gamaliel Harding*—The Macmillan Co., 1965

Starling, Col. Edmund W.—*Starling of the White House*—Simon & Schuster, 1946

West, J.B.—*42 Years in the White House*—Houghton Mifflin, 1934
Presidential site: Marion, OH: http://www.hardinghome.org/

Grace Goodhue Coolidge

Lathem, Edw. C. (ed)—*Meet Calvin Coolidge*—Stephen Greene, 1960

Ross, Ishbel—*Grace Coolidge and Her Era*—Dodd Mead, 1962

Schlaes, Amity—*Coolidge*—Harper Collins, 2013

Starling, Col. Edmund W.—*Starling of the White House*—Simon & Schuster, 1946

West, J.B.—*42 Years in the White House*—Houghton Mifflin, 1934

Wikander, Lawrence and Ferrel, Robt. (eds.)—*Grace Coolidge: An Autobiography*—High Plains Publishing, 1982

Presidential site: Plymouth Notch, VT: http://www.nps.gov/nr/travel/presidents/calvin_coolidge_homestead.html

Lou Henry Hoover

Mayer, Dale C. (ed.)—*Lou Henry Hoover: Essays*—High Plains Publishing, 1994

Peare, Catherine O.—*The Herbert Hoover Story*—Thomas Y. Crowell, 1965

Pryor, Dr. Helen B.—*Lou Henry Hoover: Gallant First Lady*—Dodd Mead, 1969

West, J.B.—*42 Years in the White House*—Houghton Mifflin, 1934

Presidential site: West Branch, IA: http://hoover.archives.gov/

Anna Eleanor Roosevelt Roosevelt

Brands, H.W.—*Traitor to His Class*—Doubleday, 2008

Burns, James and Dunn, Susan—*The Three Roosevelts*—Atlantic Monthly, 2001

Cook, Blanche Wiesen—*Eleanor Roosevelt: Vol 1—1884-1933*—Viking, 1992

– *Eleanor Roosevelt: Vol 2: 1933-1938*—Penguin, 1999

Goodwin, Doris Kearns—*No Ordinary Time*—Simon & Schuster, 1994

Halsey, William F. & Bryan, J. III—*Admiral Halsey's Story*—McGraw Hill, 1947

Harrity, R. & Martin R.—*Eleanor Roosevelt: Her Life in Pictures*—Duell, Sloan & Pearce, 1958

Lash, Joseph—*Eleanor and Franklin*—W.W. Norton, 1986

– *Eleanor Roosevelt: A Friend's Memoir*—Doubleday & Co., 1964

Nesbitt, Henrietta—*White House Diary*—Doubleday & Co., 1948

Pottker, Jan—*Sara and Eleanor*—St. Martin's Press, 2004

Roosevelt, Eleanor—*The Autobiography of Eleanor Roosevelt*—Harper & Bros. 1961

Presidential sites: Hyde Park, NY: http://www.nps.gov/hofr/index.htm

http://www.fdrlibrary.marist.edu/archives/collections/franklin/

First Lady site: Hyde Park, NY: http://www.nps.gov/elro/index.htm

Bess Wallace Truman

Ferrell, Robt. H. (ed.)—*Dear Bess: Letters From Harry*—W.W. Norton, 1983

McCullough, David—*Truman*—Simon & Schuster, 1992

Miller, Merle—*Plain Speaking*—Berkley Publishing, 1974

Sale, Sara L—*Bess Wallace Truman*—University Press of Kansas, 2010

Truman, Margaret—*Harry W. Truman*—William Morrow, 1972

– *Bess W. Truman*—Macmillan, 1986

– *Where The Buck Stops*—Warner, 1969

Presidential site: Independence, MO: http://www.trumanlibrary.org/

http://www.nps.gov/hstr/index.htm

http://www.trumanlittlewhitehouse.com/

Mamie Doud Eisenhower

Brandon, Dorothy—*Mamie Doud Eisenhower*—Scribners, 1954

Eisenhower, David and Eisenhower, Julie Nixon—*Going Home to Glory*—Simon & Schuster, 2010

Eisenhower, Dwight D.—*Letters to Mamie*—Doubleday, 1978

Eisenhower, Susan—*Mrs. Ike*—Farrar Straus Giroux, 1996

Lester, David and Lester, Irene—*Ike and Mamie*—G.P. Putnam, 1981

Perret, Geoffrey—*Eisenhower*—Random House, 1999

Presidential sites: Abilene, KS: http://www.eisenhower.archives.gov/
Gettysburg, PA: http://www.nps.gov/eise/index.htm